FAMILY CONNECTIONS

FAMILY CONNECTIONS

Parenting Your Grown Children

ARTHUR MASLOW, M.S.W.,
and MOIRA DUGGAN

FOREWORD BY
DONALD A. BLOCH, M.D.

1982
DOUBLEDAY & COMPANY, INC.
GARDEN CITY, NEW YORK

ISBN: 0-385-17094-7
LIBRARY OF CONGRESS CATALOG CARD NUMBER 81–43010
COPYRIGHT © 1982 BY ARTHUR MASLOW AND MOIRA DUGGAN
ALL RIGHTS RESERVED
PRINTED IN THE UNITED STATES OF AMERICA
FIRST EDITION

To all my family, without whose help
there would be no book: especially
Barbara, Liz, and Tom, who made it
possible for me to be a parent;
Carol, Toni, and Mark, who aided in my
education; and my professional "family,"
whose help has been indispensable.

———————

To Sheila and Bob Miller

FOREWORD

Readers of this fine book will receive at least three major benefits. They will be introduced to an important new way of understanding families, known as the "family-systems approach"; they will be introduced as well to some of the newest concepts and techniques for accomplishing family change; and, finally, they will learn what a wise and experienced professional has to say about that essential but little-noticed aspect of parenthood, the continuation of parenting into the child's late adolescent and adult years. All of these topics have been the subject of intense professional interest in recent years, yet there has been little or no attention paid to them in media accessible to the general public.

In the past, most books about being a parent dealt with the first few years of life; some went on to consider the problems of the adolescent stage. There seemed to be a general assumption that parenting responsibilities ended there, although such a notion flies in the face of our common experience. After all, the majority of those who read this book are either the parents of adult children or the adult children of parents. Or both. Speaking for myself, I belong in both categories; my mother is in her eighties and my older children are in their twenties. Not a day goes by that I am not aware of the living ties between us that are potentially a rich and nourishing source of strength and goodness, or—on rare occasions, fortunately—the source of the most dismal and painful discomfort. My mother and my children are not the only reference points in my life—

not my only "significant others"—but they are steadily and consistently of consequence to me. My mother still mothers me, and in my adult life we have had the chance to continue working and sorting out many issues that were only partially dealt with in my earlier, growing-up years. The same is true for my three adult children. We struggle forward bit by bit, doing well most of the time and trying to make up for it when we don't.

One of the reasons that popular literature has not included books such as this one is that it is only in the last decade or so that scientists and professionals in the mental health field have been paying significant attention to the idea that human development continues past the mid-twenties. Today, much study and research goes into the effort to understand the nature of our passage through the middle and later years.

The scientific study of the family as a *system*, rather than as a mere collection of individuals, is also a comparatively recent arrival among students of human behavior. According to this approach, family therapists treat mental health problems in the context of the family rather than as the isolated difficulties of individuals. It has taught us to pay close attention to the march of the generations and the links between them; in particular, it has taught us to look at this process as it continues well past early childhood.

It is this systems approach to families that the authors present in this book. They have recapitulated these advances and rendered them understandable and interesting to the lay reader. In the course of doing so they touch upon many problems that are familiar to us all, dealing in turn with the early transitional years and then going on to consider various problems of separation and autonomy on the one hand and continued connection on the other. The book is full of practical information on negotiating these issues that will be of considerable benefit to careful readers. Beyond that, it is informed by a perspective on life and the family that is bound to be a source of comfort, strength, and occasionally laughter.

Donald A. Bloch, M.D.

CONTENTS

INTRODUCTION

There are signs that our culture is on the threshold of a new understanding of the family. Just as the 1960s saw an awakening to concepts of ecological systems in nature, and the 1970s were a time of intense popular and scientific interest in the solar system, so the 1980s promise to be a time of awareness and inquiry into that human constellation we call the family, which has been until now one of the most common and least understood of human institutions. The trend should bring greater knowledge of how and why families begin, how they endure, and what really transpires behind the events that are common to families everywhere.

This book is written in hopes of shedding light on that stage in family life when relationships are coming full circle: when parents, after devoting their middle years to the creation of a family, are being liberated—often with mixed feelings—from the cares and tasks of raising their children; when those children themselves, after making their emancipation moves, are moving toward the responsibilities of partnership and parenthood.

The forces at work during this time are powerful, being wielded as they are by adult wills and capabilities. In many households, parents and their postadolescent children interact in ways that are fraught with resentment, guilt, bewilderment—all part of the process of separation.

Our goal in this book is to give parents and their grown children a new way of looking at the interactions and events of this time. The issues and problematical situations discussed are those one can expect to encounter in the average family. Understand, however, that bizarre-seeming things happen in "average" families. What you and I may look on as aberrant behavior may work very well for the family down the block. Thus, we do not speak here of "norms" but of *workability*.

When patterns of living are not working, when a family feels troubled, ill at ease, locked into a network of unhelpful dependencies, then this is the time for a family to consider the need for and the possibilities of change. What favors the betterment of problem situations is this extraordinary fact about family life, something I have seen demonstrated in my life and practice and which I believe with my heart and soul: it is that no one—parent or child—ever does less than the best job that he or she can do. The family is a system, an ever-evolving, changing, completely well-balanced entity. Its members never seek to harm or destroy the family; on the contrary, whatever they do represents their best efforts to keep their family system in balance. This phenomenon, which is extremely complex, has been explained clinically in books for family therapy professionals. This book attempts to explain it in terms that families can easily relate to their own lives. It contains the sometimes random thoughts of a family-systems therapist —a businessman turned psychotherapist—who has made his work that of helping family members lead lives of their own while remaining securely anchored in family relationships that are comfortable and not restrictive.

A.M.

In a book collaboration, it is necessary to decide at the outset on the authorial voice. Of the possible choices, *we* would not have been appropriate, since the book is essentially the outgrowth of the experience of the family-therapist author (Arthur Maslow). It seemed best, therefore, to use *I* and *we* as they fell naturally in the text, the *I* referring to Arthur Maslow, the *we* referring to both authors speaking jointly.

Also, although we have used the pronoun *he* when referring to both sexes, it is not to be understood as an endorsement of this one-sided usage. The choice was made because alternate twinning of pronouns for absolute fairness ("he or she," "his or hers," "she or he," "hers or his") proves impossibly unwieldy in sentences of more than one clause. We have tried, nevertheless, to be as evenhanded as possible in gender references. We hope that our position will be more tellingly revealed in the content of the book, which is written on the premise that sexual inequality has no place in the future of the family.

M.D.

FAMILY CONNECTIONS

1
UNDERSTANDING
THE FAMILY

"I hate them," the woman said with an explosive laugh. She was somewhere in her fifties, carefully coiffed and dressed, a community leader. And she was speaking about her two sons, one nineteen, the other twenty-one. Now that they were growing up, living with them was supposed to be easier. Instead, she felt that things were falling apart, that nothing would work out as she had hoped.

Talking with her roommate, Paula, age twenty-eight, was indignant. "When I had lunch with my mother yesterday," she said, "she wasn't even nice enough to ask me about my job!" In a nearby suburb meanwhile, Paula's mother was confiding to a friend, "If we ask Paula anything about her life she accuses us of prying, so we've decided to stay out of things and keep the peace. When I had lunch with her yesterday, I didn't ask her a single question about her job!"

The executive sat back for a moment of non-business chat. "There's just one thing I can't seem to handle," he said. "My kids." He began to recount the troubles that made him almost dread going home at night: a teenage daughter who alternately starved and gorged herself, another who'd been taken down to the police station for smoking pot

outside the local elementary school. "We've tried everything,"
he said. "We don't know what else to do."

Why would a mother say, even facetiously, of her children, "I hate them"? Why would a young woman and her
mother find it so difficult to communicate? Why does a
loving and concerned father find himself powerless to help
his troubled children?

None of these families is especially unusual. If we look
into our own families, each of us will find some degree of
discomfort somewhere in our family relationships. Like the
people above, we may wish to be free of that sense of dis-
ease, to resolve outstanding issues and put our family relationships on a more comfortable basis, but we find this
very difficult to do.

The main reason why we find it hard to change and to
evolve new ways of relating is that we lack a true understanding of how the family works. We tend to think of the
family as something made up of a mother, father, and
child (or children), with aunts, uncles, and cousins. And
that definition is correct as far as it goes. But in reality the
family is a system—to be sure, a system much smaller than
the solar system and much larger than, say, the human re-
spiratory system, but a system that is in its way just as
complex and fully integrated as these. It is this systemic operation of the family, and how it affects relationships between parents and their grown children, that we hope to
explain here and in the chapters to come.

· A New Family Forms

As practice in thinking of the family as a system, suppose we look at a typical simple family cycle and follow, in

An important stage in a family system. A boy from one family and a girl from another fall in love, marry, and begin their own family. Parents, siblings, aunts, uncles, cousins are all part of the enlarged family system.

broad outline, its systemic developments over the course of a generation.

John is the oldest child of parents who have been married for thirty years. His father has earned a modest living as an electrician; a few years ago, his mother returned to paid work in the office of an elementary school. John is now twenty-three and has three younger siblings, a boy and two girls. By dint of hard work and frugal living, his parents have been able to give him the advantage of a college education and he is now in his first job as a management trainee for the telephone company.

John is in love with a girl named Mary. She is twenty-two, the daughter of a lawyer father and a mother who is a buyer in one of the city's larger department stores. Her family lives in a house in one of the quiet residential enclaves of the city; they have always been well-off financially and they pursue an active social life. Mary, after getting her BA at a small New England women's college, is training to work as a guidance counselor. She met John six months ago, and now the two have decided they want to get married.

As the marriage of John and Mary approaches, their families need to come together in some way. Each family has to "let go" of an offspring so that the two will be free to marry and start a family of their own. At the same time, each family has to open up sufficiently to accept a partner for their child. The result is that the two families become linked.

John's family accepts Mary as a daughter-in-law and gives her a place together with the other children. Her position may in a sense be "higher" than theirs, "lower" than theirs, closer to the parents, or farther away—any of these positions is possible. The same is true of John as he enters Mary's family. He could be put on a level with her, or he could be put on a sort of test platform where he would

to deal with the void his absence has created in her
Some of these hours she spends in school-related activ-
; the rest of the time she fills with activities not related
immy.

As Jimmy gets older, he moves farther out into the
rld. His peers, his teachers, and others take on greater
portance in his life, while his parents are more and more
cluded. One day, shortly after turning nineteen, Jimmy
aves his parents and goes off to college 1,500 miles away
om home. John and Mary now have to try to reshape
heir relationship with each other and come to terms with
life that is suddenly empty of the daily tasks and pas-
imes of child-rearing. This is less of a problem for John,
who now has a demanding executive position with his
company. However, Mary, after a year's "vacation," feels
restless, so she goes back to school to complete her training
as a guidance counselor.

While Jimmy is at college, he keeps in touch with his
parents pretty faithfully by letter. He also spends a lot of
his free time in the home of his uncle Bill, who lives with
his wife and three children in a suburb not far from
Jimmy's college. In his senior year Jimmy tells his parents
that he would like to go on to law school and his parents
agree happily, for they are pleased to see him following in
his grandfather's footsteps.

Jimmy goes on to law school and does well. In his final
year he writes to John and Mary that he and the girl he's
been dating for a year have decided to get married as soon
as he has passed his bar exam and gotten a job. John and
Mary view the impending marriage with some reservations,
thinking that perhaps their son should wait until he is
more established in his career. But they have no intention
of opposing the marriage; they have met the girl and like
her, and in the back of their minds they wouldn't mind

have to prove himself, coming as he (
cial and economic stratum than Mary':

While this process is taking place,
ried young people start to form their
tionship. They have to learn to live w
make their complementary parts work to
basis of a lasting relationship. While dc
also interacting with the other members
families. In this case, all goes well, and sc
system is created that encompasses the m
and Mary, which is itself a new system in
stages of formation.

When their baby is born, a year after the
John and Mary's little system is considera
They call the baby Jimmy, after Mary's fa
makes a big change in their lives. Up to no\
been a twosome; now they are a threesome. Ma
have to move apart from each other a little to
in their lives for Jimmy. As is true in most fa
child occupies a position that is somewhat clo
mother than to his father—mainly because his firs
contact is with her and she does most of the c
him.

As an infant, Jimmy is dependent on his paren
full twenty-four hours a day. All he can do for hir
breathe and move about a little. When he starts t
and talk it is in ways that are patterned by what h
and hears around him—ways that fit in with the 1
norms.

When he is five years old Jimmy starts going to scl
it is his first significant step outward from his infant p
tion in the family. Now, for several hours during the d
he is in the care of other people and Mary finds that s

has
life.
ities
to

wo
im
ex
le
fr
tl
a
t

having their lives peopled by the addition of a daughter-in-law and perhaps in time a grandchild or two.

We will leave this family at this point. It's a fairly prosaic story and in order to see its relevance we have to read between the lines.

The story shows, first of all, how marriage forms a connection between two otherwise unconnected families, thereby creating an enlarged family system. It illustrates the way complementarity can work in attracting people to one another: Mary seeing in John something she had missed in her own family—the presence of siblings and a livelier, less formal home atmosphere; John seeing in Mary a bridge to social and economic betterment. The story also illustrates how spatial relationships change in the course of a family's history: a certain distance opening between the parents as they make room for their child in their relationship; the gradual move of the child out of that position into the world, allowing the parents to move closer again as they try to fill the space vacated by the child. Again, the story illustrates how a family pattern can be transmitted; in this case, Jimmy's being influenced by his respect for his grandfather in choosing to follow the same profession and in choosing to marry early in life, as his parents did. It illustrates, further, how the family can provide a comforting sense of connectedness in the way that Jimmy, while far from home, is able to feel at home in his uncle's household. Finally, the story shows how freedom from excessive dependency allows all the members of the family to grow and change: for the child to leave home at the appropriate time, for the mother to find a satisfying outlet for her energies, for the father—being thus unburdened—to continue to progress in his own work.

Perhaps readers are thinking that their own family has

nothing in common with the family I have just described. But let's look at it again.

Your family, like the family of John and Mary, is a structure. It has parts (members) in a framework of relationships.

Your family, like theirs, is a mechanism. Its members mesh and interact with each other, and each relationship between family members affects the system as a whole.

Most important, your family, like the family we have just described, keeps itself in a kind of balance. Everyone, though they may not be conscious of it, reacts to events in the life of the family in ways that are designed to keep the family from disintegrating. Just as nature abhors a vacuum, the family abhors disintegration.

Here we are entering on the difficult subject of family equilibrium, or *homeostasis*, as it is called in the fields of social science.

The System in Operation

To understand homeostasis, it may be helpful to compare the family to some of the systems we are more familiar with. Think, for example, of a heating system that clicks on when the temperature in a house falls below the setting on the thermostat. The thermostat reacts, causing the furnace to go on, which supplies warm air to bring the temperature in the house back into the comfortable range. Families, too, have their "thermostats." When there is a change for "better" or "worse," the members of a family sense a rising or falling level of comfort and they respond in ways that are available to them at that time. To the outside world, these ways don't always seem appropriate, but they are the ways that fit in with the pushes and pulls at work in the system. By "pushes and pulls" I mean such factors as the personalities of the family members (both present and remembered), the alliances that exist among them, the patterns of frustration or gratification in their lives, and events they experience.

Like all systems, the family is always undergoing change; it is never static. Birth, death, and the stages between; marriage and divorce; household moves and job changes—all this is the stuff of family life. We might even say that the "work" of the family is continual adjustment to change. Whenever one of these stresses occurs, the family reacts in ways that will bring the system back into a workable balance.

For example, when a father is suddenly taken out of the family system due to death or divorce, the rest of the family will move to "fill in" for the absent father. The mother may step into the role of the breadwinner; the children will try to take care of their mother's needs—or what they perceive to be her needs now that she is in some way incomplete.

In the family, as with all systems, this elasticity is possible because the system is made up of parts that co-vary with each other and no one part is able to govern or manipulate the system as a whole.

As members of a family, we are to some extent limited in our freedom to act; we are in a real sense caught up in the life of the system. The ways we act in response to change are unconscious behaviors for maintaining the family equilibrium. We do what is *possible*, though it may not always seem logical or rational. And whatever we do represents our best efforts to preserve the family.

This phenomenon of homeostasis is the reason why, in dealing with family problems, we must first set aside the idea that someone in the family—ourself or someone else—is to blame for the trouble. Blame is simply not a valid concept in the systemic view of family.

In the course of this book we will discuss some of the equilibrating moves commonly experienced in families where children are coming of age and moving out into lives of their own. The point to grasp at the outset is that problems do not exist in isolation; they are part of the family's balancing act. *All behaviors are attempts to preserve the family, never to destroy it.*

Behaviors

You might respond, "It's all fine to say that no one's to blame, but can you explain why our child is causing us such worry and heartache?"

I often hear questions like this from parents as they describe their child's troublesome behavior—which can be anything from vandalism, alcoholism, school problems, drug-taking, running away, dropping out, losing jobs, or perhaps nothing worse than simply preferring to look sloppy all the time. I tell these families that the way to begin finding the answer is to rephrase the question. The question is not "Why is our child doing this to us?" The question is, *"Why is this happening to us?"*

What family members need to understand is that in families there is no such thing as individual behavior. There is only family behavior. The way a child behaves is dictated by the needs of the family equilibrium. A child will do only as well or as badly as his family can stand. Now, this is not to say that if Johnny is coming home from school stoned every day, or if Susie keeps running away, that his or her parents are responsible. Parents do not cause their children's behavior any more than children cause their parents' behavior. Nevertheless, it is true that everyone in the family is part of the mechanical operation of the family. They all act and they all *re*act to each other's actions.

The phase we are discussing in this book—when the children are passing from childhood dependency to the maturity of adulthood—is rarely a serene period in family life. On the contrary, it tends to be a time of troublesome behaviors that can cause discomfort and bewilderment to everyone.

The concept of the family system has brought helpful insights into this difficult phase. To begin with, it helps explain family members' seemingly disruptive behaviors. These are not "bad" behaviors; they are merely the behaviors that are available to the family at that particular time for maintaining the family's homeostasis. It is for this reason that we look on all behaviors—the "good" and the "bad"—as attempts at constructive action.

Every family has its own way of behaving that sets it apart from every other family. Some families function well and easily, and at the other end of the spectrum there are families that seem to function in a constant state of near disaster.

I am often asked what it is that sets the so-called healthy and well-functioning families apart from the rest. It is certainly not that they enjoy especially good luck; like all families, they have their share of accidents and reversals. What does seem to set them apart is the ability of the members to evolve a balance of interdependencies. They remain to some extent dependent on one another as parts of the same family system, yet they are also independent as individuals. They cooperate to maintain the family equilibrium, but there is a physical and emotional distance between the parents and their grown children that allows the members of both generations to grow and to develop their

individuality. When we hear complaints that signal dysfunction and dis-ease in families, such as "Why is our
child doing this to us?" it usually means that this process
of growth and distancing is not going very well.

In any case, family behavior is not a magical thing. It
can be understood, described, and even changed.

Family Change

We are constantly having to adjust to change in our
lives. Seasons turn, prices go up, friends and relatives die,
we grow older, and so on. This kind of change is largely beyond our control. There is another kind of change, however, over which we do have a measure of control. It is the
kind of change people have in mind when they say, "I
wish things were different." In many cases, the
"difference" is something they have the power to bring
about themselves: a change from painful patterns of living
to less painful patterns of living.

Although this kind of change is possible, unfortunately
the difficulties in achieving it are tremendous. We tend to
cling to what we know, even when we are miserable living
with the known. When we try to think of an alternative,
all we see is an empty space in the future, and a void like
that is more frightening than a present situation in which
we are at least surviving.

Nevertheless, people can and do change. They say to
themselves, "I understand what I have been doing and I
know that I have to take steps to change my life," then
they bring to bear all their resources—cognitive, emotional,
and behavioral—in order to do things differently. In families, this means a shared effort. There has to be a willingness on the part of each member to say "I want the system
to change and I will do all I can to accomplish this."

Today many Americans are trying to change their lives in the belief that they can be or do anything they want so long as they motivate themselves to achieve that goal. This prescription, preached by many in the self-help movement, takes little or no account of the ever-present family system. It would be more realistic to say that you can be or do whatever you want so long as your family system can accept your being something different from what you are and have been. Your change can happen only if the other people in your system also change in some way so that the system is able to rebalance.

The more deeply established a family pattern, the harder it is to change. Of course, there are catastrophic events that change families overnight, but normally the process of change and growth is very slow, added to bit by bit over a long period of time. The differences are so minute from day to day and week to week that families are tempted to give up their efforts. The worst pitfall is that as families begin to change, often they find that they still feel miserable and so they give up the ground they have gained and go back to where they were before; they don't give the change time to become established and comfortable in their lives. I sometimes see this happen in family therapy situations where parents are being encouraged to try new ways of interacting with their children: if they don't see a startling, immediate difference they give up the idea even though it was already bringing about a slight improvement in the situation.

To repeat, individuals and families cannot change in a short period of time. The system needs time to incorporate the differences; members need time to react differently and to accept the newness in their lives. The increments need time to build. Gradually the obstacles to change erode away. The frightening unknown—that empty space in our future—becomes a reality. We come to see that we can even change our past, since what we do today and in the days that follow becomes a part of our past as soon as we have done it. It is as if we were weavers working at the loom of life. We work in different threads and gradually we create a pattern of different colors and textures, which is to say, we create a past of a different content and meaning in our lives.

Testing the System at the Time of Separation

If you are the parents of a young person who is making his or her moves toward independence, it may be of some comfort to you to know that these moves are of their very nature *oppositional*. Many parents think that the atmosphere of turbulence that accompanies separation must be due to some sort of mismanagement on their part. The truth is, no matter how well you manage things as a parent, you never seem to win with a teenager. The young person is testing the atmosphere for leaving, which means that he is creating an emotional and perhaps also a physical void in the place he has occupied for something like two decades in the life of the family system. He tests in tentative ways at first, spending more time in the company of peers and activities that exclude his parents; he may do things that go directly against his parents' wishes. No matter what form his testing takes, however, his actual separation can only happen if the system is able to adjust and rebalance itself in response to the change.

It takes considerable wisdom on the part of parents to recognize that their child's seemingly negative behaviors can be signs of growth. (This is not to say that all oppositional behaviors indicate the process of maturation. Sometimes they are the child's way of dealing with some other problem in the life of the family.) In any case, parents have to realize that growing up is a progression of decisions, some of which are well taken and some are mistaken; it is not a sudden and magical assumption of adulthood.

Naturally, during this phase parents want to be just as loving and protective of their children as they were when the children were young. But they should understand that their self-liberating child doesn't need them to take the role of social director, godlike adviser, or knower of right and wrong. Precisely because the young person is trying to separate and test the parameters of life, almost anything the parents say if they involve themselves in this kind of decision-making is going to be wrong—that is, perceived by the child as wrong.

We tend to underestimate, I think, the patience and faith that parents need in order to let the separation moves take place. Besides feeling almost assaulted by their child's behavior, many parents carry with them the germ of fear that they are going to feel lonely once their children are gone. This fear is natural and to some extent justified. But in a well-differentiated family, where the members are "dependently independent," the ties can be expected to remain in effect over time and space after separation has occurred. We don't cease to be parents after our children have grown up, we simply become the parents of grown-ups. And as for children, I think the truth of the matter is that none of them wishes to be completely cut off from his or her family. Indeed, parenting is an endless responsibility (some would call it a bottomless pit). It never ends.

The chapters ahead will try to provide insights into the process of offspring separation. They proceed generally in chronological order through the later stages of emancipation: from the late teen years and the early self-liberating moves, to the stage of liberation for offspring *and* parents.

Among the topics addressed are: limit-setting (how much and how to do it); money (handling it fairly and responsibly); sex (especially questions raised by the *mores* of our time); school performance (parental pressures on students; possible hidden messages behind dropping out and failing); life decisions (how and how not to help your children); emotional difficulties (dealing with depression, flakiness, antisocial behavior, and the fear some young people have about leaving home).

The book does not offer manipulative ploys for parents to use with their grown children. It concentrates on showing the underlying dynamics of family interaction. Readers who see similarities between their lives and the situations that are discussed may come to a better understanding of what is happening in their own family systems. Most of all, our aim is to give readers a new way of looking at themselves and their families. For some families this will mean owning up to the existence of a problem. It's much easier to deny our problems, to say that everything's fine. If we admitted the problem, then we would feel burdened by the need to change. Yet the other path—failing to take steps to change—is even more dangerous, since the problem that isn't dealt with may become a part of the family's functioning. The members may integrate the problem into their daily life and grow to need it as a necessary element of the family homeostasis.

As part of the effort they make to see their family with fresh eyes, we ask parents to dispense with the notion of blame and accept that every behavior, no matter how bizarre, is a helping behavior, something the family member does for the purpose of maintaining the family system.

I can hear some parent exclaiming, "What! My kid is taking uppers and downers and sidewayers and whatever he can get his hands on. How is that helping the family?"

That parent's worry and distress are justified, but as long as he is focusing on the "problem" he will not get the answer he seeks. That can only be gained by looking at the complete systemic picture—including home, school, peers, and certainly the parents themselves and their marriage.

This may sound like the approach that any rational family would take in a problem situation, yet it rarely happens this way, because this approach—the systemic approach—allows no room for that classic psychological crutch, the scapegoat. It is very hard to accept that all the members of a family—ourselves included—are doing the best job they can. But once we accept this truth, we are free to act toward one another from loving motives, not from motives of guilt or anger.

Some Principles of Family Peace

We will come back again and again to certain basic principles that apply in all areas and all stages of parent-child interaction—whether it has to do with the child's first serious love, his school achievements, his choice of career, or any of the other events or developments in the process of growing up.

One of these principles has to do with *reexamining attitudes toward experimentation, limit-setting, and standards.* The time of coming of age is particularly rife with conflict over these matters. Some parents seem born with the wisdom to let their children take risks; perhaps they know from their own youthful experience that we learn more from failure than we do from success. If their child fails or makes a mistake, they don't allow it to become a source of family shame. Such parents set very few rules, but the rules they set are reasonable and sincere, and as their children become more and more self-reliant, they have no difficulty phasing out these rules and accepting their children, finally, as adults. Most of us parents are not so clear and confident, however. We may live within a set of strictures that help us to feel secure, and if we try to apply these various "shoulds" to our grown children, the process of emancipation can't go smoothly.

Thinking the Unthinkable is a helpful approach to be tried on seemingly intractable problems. (For example, your daughter, eighteen, is dressing like a ragamuffin and is a slob around the house. You want to scream. Instead, offer to have the family move out of the house so that she'll have it all to herself and discuss with her how this radical step can be made.) Thinking the Unthinkable is an exercise designed to wake us up to the reality that in any situation there are virtually unlimited choices available to us so long as we can begin to think about them, and our thinking about them should go as far afield as possible from the actual problem. In seeking solutions, then, we can start with the Unthinkable and move from there to alternatives that are possible even if extreme or surprising.

Another principle to observe in settling family issues is *to preserve equality among family members according to their place in the family hierarchy*. If the interests of many are sacrificed to the interests of one, it can only pull the system out of balance and create family discomfort. (An example might be the family that scrimps and denies itself in order to send a son or daughter to college while asking another child to go to work at age sixteen.)

Having realistic expectations and aspirations is another underlying principle of family peace. A family in thrall to some stereotypical view of what it should be will be prone to disruptive tensions. The test seems to be whether expectations are realistic or unrealistic. Pressures to achieve may be quite realistic in a family that has a tradition of professional, mercantile, or artistic achievement. Unrealistic expectations, on the other hand, often spring from the parents' wishes to see their children live out their own unfulfilled dreams, and the reaction to such expectations is often perverse. The children end up having and doing less; or if they do achieve, they do it without zest.

The subject of family communication is discussed in a separate chapter. However, one principle of effective communication is so fundamental to family peace that it comes up repeatedly throughout this book. We have tried to describe it visually, as the *side-by-side approach*. If two people look at a problem together, as if they were standing shoulder to shoulder instead of eyeball to eyeball, it is almost impossible for fighting and estrangement to develop between those people. What happens so often in family life (and in every area of our lives) is that people express their thoughts and feelings in ways that cause any difference of opinion to become deeply entrenched; the issue may either be given up as "lost" (that is, it becomes incorporated into the family's way of operating), or it becomes a constant irritant. Side-by-side discussion helps prevent this from happening.

"Tethering"

The family in some form or another is here to stay; it is inescapable. It is something we all need as a source of strength and stability in our lives. But there is no guarantee that the family will function in this way. Sometimes the dependencies that are an inevitable part of family life become so rooted that they prevent family members from

The simple two-ness of the newly married couple ends when their baby is born, and family unity is challenged as the child enters adolescence. It's often hard for parents to understand that their child's risk-taking and oppositional behaviors are part of the process of growing up.

individuating and becoming persons in their own right. We have to try to avoid this, to deal with the interdependencies so that they work in helpful, cooperative ways for the people involved.

This process, whereby we become *dependently independent*, is the real goal of family life. More than that, it seems to be a prerequisite for any happiness we hope to enjoy as emancipated people. The story of a family should build up to satisfactions for everyone in return for the love and effort that have gone into it. A family story that ends in disconnection and nostalgia for a lost sense of belonging is a sad story indeed.

There is a curious paradox in the process of offspring separation. It is that a sense of connectedness is more liberating than a sense of isolation or severance from family. I think of this connectedness as something like the tether that keeps a spacewalker vitally connected to his ship, secure in the void of the universe. Everyone should have a "tether." It is our link to the essentials of life. Without it we fly off.

2

THE TRANSITIONAL YEARS

The transitional years—from adolescence to maturity—
might be called the noisy years. A lot of roaring goes on.

I think of an old lion and his offspring, a young lion
who is growing up and feeling frisky. One day the young
lion roars at his father and looks to see if it makes the old
lion flinch. Then he behaves himself for a while; he eats
some carcasses and gets bigger, and on another day gives a
louder roar and maybe advances a step to see if the old
lion holds his ground. Finally the day comes when he
swats his daddy on the nose and walks away from the pride
to live in a territory of his own.

In some ways that's what young people do when they
make their independence moves. They make their tests,
one after another, in an escalating series that shows
whether or not the young person is ready to leave and
whether the family is ready to let him go.

Where this analogy falls short is in the suggestion that
human beings mature the way the other animals do—at
certain predictable ages. This is not so. Although we need

to transit from adolescence to physical and emotional maturity, there is no finite transition period as such. The transition starts at a different age for each individual.

Nevertheless, in our culture we tend to equate maturity with events that are supposed to happen at particular points in life. For example, we hear parents say, "My kid is twenty-five and still living at home!" "I don't know why my son isn't married by now!" "If my daughter doesn't have a baby by the time she's thirty, she might as well forget it!" And, unfortunately, for those young people who are having trouble reaching maturity, despairing comments of this sort made by their parents, teachers, and other authority figures only make the transition harder.

The Nature of Independence Moves

In trying to understand what it means to "grow up," and why that transition doesn't necessarily happen in step with the physical maturation of a young person, we should keep in mind that whatever happens in families is part of their homeostasis—of the way they keep themselves in equilibrium. The transition takes place when the family allows it to happen. The movement might occur at any time from the early teens to a point much later in life; for some the transition never comes. In step with the child's move to adulthood there comes a change also in the parents' role. They go from parenting a dependent child to parenting an independent adult, and when they no longer have children who are dependent on them, they need to fill the void in their lives with other things.

We are talking here about the interaction between parents and children that occurs during the transitional years, as the child ceases to be a responder to limits set down by others and becomes an initiator of his or her own limits.

The young person tries to enlarge his authority and experience as the parents try to open up and remove their controls. It is a very delicate time.

In calling the transitional years the noisy years, I am not referring just to the decibels and soundwaves that are so much a part of this time. I am referring, rather, to a quality that is characteristic of adolescence.

Adolescents are like energy fields, and the energy they give off is often felt by adults as something disruptive, dangerous, anxiety-producing. Adults cannot simply ignore this quality. It's like sharing a bus seat with a very fat person. When adolescents come into a room, the amount of space they occupy is almost always more than the space occupied by their physical being or the space occupied by an adult of the same size. That "fatness" of the adolescent pushes against adults and forces them to move in some way.

The energy of adolescence isn't always expressed in activity, however; it can also take the opposite form: depression and an inability to communicate.

Parents are sometimes unsure about how to respond to adolescent energy. When children are small, if they become frenetic and start running around, it is simple to hold them for a while until they quiet down. But you can't grab a teenager and hold him till he quiets down (although some programs for disturbed teenagers do use this approach). One positive way adults can respond is to give adolescents the extra "space" they need so they will be able to operate in new ways.

What the adolescent is trying to say to his or her parents might be expressed this way: "I need space to do what I want to do. I want you to be confident that I'm okay when I'm out on my own, just the way you are when I'm in school. I need to be able to come home later and not worry that I am disturbing you." An appropriate answer from his parents would be, "If you want us to give you space, then you need to give us a sense of security about what you do when you're on your own, the same security we feel when you're at school—that things are okay and that you're safe. You need to help us feel that you are in charge of things wherever you are."

When the transition to adulthood is going well, the teenage years should be a time when the young person is feeling more and more free and his parents are feeling more and more secure about him as he takes on increasing responsibility for his own life. Often, however, it is a time when a lot of wrenching and twisting goes on between parents and children. In many families it is marked by strife, as if the two generations were working at cross purposes with each other.

Why should this be?

In the process of emancipation the child is trying to grow up, to set his own limits and take responsibility for his own actions—as he has been told to do. But he also wants, unconsciously, to avoid harming or disturbing the family by his move from dependence to independence. So he tests the system, to see whether or not the family will be able to adjust to his leaving.

Testing the system takes any number of forms well known to parents everywhere. Basically it means that the self-emancipating young person acts in ways that are different from the norms of the parents. Different concepts of morality, different choices of friends, different modes of dress, different styles of life—these are all areas for experimentation. In the way they dress, drink, drive, study, interrelate, and so forth, young people test their family's ability to absorb change and separation.

Let's consider dress, for example. Up to a certain age a child is coiffed and clothed and bathed the way his parents think he should be. As he decides to take responsibility for his physical being, he begins to do these things his own way. A few years ago long hair was the style for young males; today many in the youth culture are chopping their hair off. Either style may affront the norms of one or both parents. Imagine that Mr. and Mrs. Jones have invited his mother for Thanksgiving dinner. They've dressed nicely for the occasion and gone to a lot of trouble to prepare a beautiful meal. When Grandma arrives, they knock on the teenager's door and out comes their son looking like a slob. Dad and Mom go bananas and the child's back gets up. Unfortunately, no one in the family is conscious of what is really going on, which is that the child is using his clothes as a symbol, as a way of showing that he is a person separate and apart from his parents; he is confused to see that it causes such anger, especially since his friends are all dressing in exactly the same way.

Family Dis-ease and Its Function

When a child is dressing sloppily or staying out late, or misusing his driving privileges, or doing anything else that makes the parents justifiably distressed, we have a situation in which the child is creating a state of family *dis-ease* (I use the hyphen here to restrict the meaning of the word to a "lack of emotional ease"). Dis-ease is the atmosphere that surrounds conflict, and it is often more readily sensed than the conflict itself or the circumstances that are causing the conflict. This kind of dis-ease is the norm during the phase of family life we are discussing. It is, and should be, a very functional state, and it should be looked on as a positive factor in evolving family relationships—no less positive than contentment and ease. *Dis-ease is something that seems negative but which actually exists for positive rea-*

sons. It is dysfunctional only when it reaches a level that overwhelms the family. Here is an example of dis-ease operating in a typical family situation.

Harvey Morris is at odds with his seventeen-year-old son Keith over what time the boy should be home at night. In order to arrive at a resolution of the hours question, Keith has to make his father dis-eased about it (something he does unconsciously). He has to demonstrate what *he* thinks the outer limits are, and so on several occasions he comes in around four o'clock in the morning.

If Keith were to stay within his father's proposed limit—eleven-thirty—then Keith would be dis-eased by that. However, in the family system, a parent does not want his child to feel dis-eased any more than he himself wants to feel dis-eased. In this situation, then, the discomfort the father and son are feeling—their lack of emotional ease—helps move them toward a resolution of their conflict.

Periods of dis-ease, then, are positive signals of an area that needs to be worked on, and the actions of the child in pushing the limits are a necessary part of the movement toward resolution. Parents should try to see how their child's testing moves function in their family life, and not think of them as something designed to make their lives miserable.

When parents are unable to see their children's behaviors positively, as attempts to mature, and when they deal with those behaviors as if they *were* negative, then the family get into a situation where each side thinks the other is crazy because each side "knows" it is right. The teenager sees that he is trying to take charge of his life, as he is expected to do, but the things he does in order to take charge of his life are upsetting to his parents. The parents, for their part, have been trying to teach their child to make decisions, and now that they see him behaving in ways they think are strange, they worry that they may have created a monster.

When an issue such as hair or dress or hours becomes a constant irritant in a family, it is there for a reason, and so we try to see what that reason might be. Let's say that Chuck, age sixteen, is wearing his hair tied back in a rubber band, and his parents are divided over the way he looks. His mother likes it, and his father tells him, "You'd look a hell of a lot better if you got a haircut." The division between the parents becomes a sore in their life, with fights flaring up almost daily over the issue.

A "sore" like this is possible only when the parents have problems of their own that they have not worked out with each other. They are able to live with those problems as long as their son remains a powerful, energetic force in their lives and they have the issue of his appearance on which to focus their attention. However, the day their son moves out, the difficulties between them may begin to surface and affect their lives. If the parents aren't able to restructure their relationship, their son may come back to his old place in the family as a way of getting the marriage back to where it was.

What teenagers test, then, is not the limits their parents put on them but something much more profound: the ability of the other family members to allow a different kind of interaction with them, in which the teenagers behave as independent persons, not as the dependent persons they were as children.

How to Respond to the Testing Moves

At this juncture in the transitional years, parents may feel at something of an impasse. In earlier years they had entire responsibility for what their children did and their children saw them almost as godlike figures. Now, with their children taking on responsibility for their own lives, they wonder what their role should be.

It is not the responsibility of parents at this time to try to limit the testing moves their child makes. The limits of the testing will be applied by the teenager himself in accordance with his experience in the family up till then and with what he has learned about life from his parents, his relatives, and his entire environment. What he does in given situations will be the natural outgrowth of the way he has evolved up to that point. Teenagers who in their earlier years have been allowed to act within broad parameters rather than according to strict disciplinary rules usually fare better when the time comes for them to be self-limiting.

The difficult answer to the question, "What should parents do?" is that they should keep their limits to the minimum and specify those limits exactly.

Kids know when the rules their parents make are really Swiss cheese—as in:

"I want to go out."

"No!"

"I want to go out."

"Oh, where do you want to go?"

Here the teenager knew that the first "No" was full of holes and that the second attempt would bring out the real limit. If there was any leeway in the situation to begin with, the parent's first answer should have been something like, "Where do you want to go? Remember, we're having dinner at seven." Where there is no leeway, the answer should be "No" spoken with finality.

Decisions affecting what the teenager will do generally involve at least four influences: mother, father, teenager, and teenager's peers. And, often, when Mom, Dad, and child discuss the "right" thing for the child to do, the child's peer group—a very powerful influence in his life—is not adequately represented. What the teenager says in arguing his case with his parents often will reflect the norms of his peers, and parents who are trying to be fair will take those norms into consideration, not making them the deciding factor but not ignoring them either. If family decisions don't take peer influence into account, the teenager will find it hard to be accepted into his peers' activities and to integrate them with his role in the family.

When I see successful parenting at work in the matter of decision-making, I see a child "banging against" his parents (because that's how he finds out what the limits are), and I see the parents going into a side-by-side position with their child. In other words, these parents turn the confrontation into a discussion. They don't meet the child head to head with statements like "This is right," or "This is wrong." Instead they give the child a role in reaching a decision, and that way the child feels that he has to follow through on what he says.

It often happens that children get into activities with their peers, particularly in the use of alcohol and drugs, that cause the parents a great deal of worry. It would be, of course, heretical to suggest that children need to try drugs and alcohol in order to arrive at their own norms for functioning in society. But I have heard many parents say, "My kids are square—they've never tried anything," and in my view this represents an equally undesirable extreme if it means that those kids stay away from everything scary. Some of the most rewarding things in life are scary; they involve life and death, and the ability to handle them comes out of doing them. I don't for a second discount what we know about the sad experiences of tens of thousands of families—the auto accidents caused by drinking, the inability of young drug users to function, and so on—but the very fact of exposure to drugs and alcohol does not mean that such tragedies will ensue. I have known a great many well-functioning adults who were highly experimental as teenagers. The "experimenters" I am talking about here are the pot users, the six-pack drinkers, and so forth, not the heroin addicts or the speed freaks. In the latter situation the child is making a plea for help and the family is correct in feeling that it has to do something to help him or her. It is my experience, however, that the less dangerous forms of experimentation are likely to be resolved by the experimenters themselves, provided the family does not allow its equilibrium to be upset by the worrisome activity. As for the kids who get through the age of experimentation by floating through the cracks—by hanging back and leaving the true scope of teenage experience to their peers—I feel they may be missing out. They will never again have the chance to relive the teenage experience and to learn about life in the company of their peers.

When we ask ourselves why kids push to certain lengths in their experimentation, it is the *length* that is really in question. In our current cultural climate, a certain amount of exposure to drugs and alcohol must be expected during the transitional years. The issue is confused by emotion and by conflicting viewpoints, and often the reaction of parents in allowing family relations to be upset is more damaging to the child than the effects of using the substance, whatever it might be.

When You Absolutely Can't Stand It

A mother I know recently put to me the question, "What do you do when you absolutely *can't stand it?*"

She was referring to her son's mode of dress, and the way she phrased the question showed that she was desperate.

Desperation has to be treated as the extremely uncomfortable emotion it is, even when caused by something that others look on as a non-issue. I think issues of the kind that produce desperation are very often indicators or symptoms of a bad contract. These parents and their grown child have not established ground rules as to what is acceptable and unacceptable behavior in the family. They have not carved out a middle ground where they are able to spend comfortable time together.

When parents "can't stand" their child's behavior, they might first try to negotiate the issue. If, for example, the woman mentioned above and her husband are planning to have dinner at one of the more formal restaurants in town, she might say to her son, "We're going out to dinner tonight at George's Restaurant and we'd like you to come if you think you'd like that." Then, if Johnny wants to go, she explains, "Well, you know, it's a kind of fancy place and we'd be more comfortable if you'd wear a jacket and look different from the way you do when you come home from school every day." Johnny would say, "Well, is that a condition of my going with you?" And Mom would say, "Yes, if we go to George's it is, and tonight we are going to George's. We can go somewhere else next week where you wouldn't need to dress up, but this time we're going to George's and we'd love to have you come with us. So will you let me know?" At this point, there are no surprises about the parents' plans and Johnny can decide for himself whether or not to go. The negotiation has put Johnny in command of himself for the evening as far as dress goes and has allowed the parents to set the limits.

Now, if Johnny comes out of his room with no jacket on

and absolutely refuses to wear one, his parents can choose to go to dinner without him—although this leaves the problem unresolved. In an instance like this it is necessary to question why Johnny is refusing to put on a jacket. Usually it's because the issue has become a battlefield in the family.

One possible way to handle an issue that has become a battlefield is for the parents to deliberately call a truce, in effect, to position themselves alongside their child. According to this solution, when Johnny's parents want to have dinner with him, they go to places where his attire is the norm, and when they go to the better restaurants, he is not invited. And if he says, "I never get a chance to eat the nice meals with you," they can say, "We're sorry about that, but to eat the nice meals with us you have to dress the way we think people should be dressed in these restaurants. Otherwise we're happy to eat with you in the pizza joint."

So far, in these clashes we've described concerning dress and grooming and hygiene, the parents have been able to control the circumstances in order to spare themselves social embarrassment. Now imagine that they are having guests for a dinner party and Johnny comes out of his room wearing his torn jeans and rumpled shirt, with his hair looking like a hornet's nest, causing his parents to feel a sense of shame. What can parents do to forestall embarrassing moments like these?

I believe that young people are susceptible to reason, and a way to reason with Johnny here would be to say, "We need your cooperation. We are having the president of the bank and the assistant comptroller and my boss in to dinner tonight. Now, we know how much you don't like any pretense about dressing up, but we'd like you to work with us on the problems we have about how you would look in that kind of company. We are not arguing that you should dress up for these people, just that you help us deal with our embarrassment concerning these very formal people and your very informal way of life. What do you suggest we do, Johnny, so that we don't feel ashamed of the way you look?"

I often talk to parents who are ready to throw up their hands over some behavior of their child. They have tried reasoning with him or her—or think they have—and find themselves still mired in the battlefield with no idea of how they can resolve the issue and get free of their disease.

Often these parents have lost sight of an important fact of family life: that they are in charge of their home and that they have the right of rule-making concerning their home. A family is not a democracy. Although its members are fully equal to each other in their degree of *belonging* to the family, and although they have rights based on that equality, they do not all possess equal *authority*. To parents who say, "But our kids live here, it's their home too," my answer is, that's true as long as the kids abide by the rules that govern the way the family lives. If they don't abide by the rules, they may forfeit their rights. Remember: it is the goal of families that children grow up and leave and establish homes of their own. Those will be the homes *they* rule over.

There is no need for parents to despair in difficult situations. Within the scope of human behavior there are countless possible choices of action. When the obvious route is blocked there is always another route that will get the family where it needs to go. And to make room in the imagination for thinking about these choices, we have to begin by Thinking the Unthinkable.

If a child is unmanageable, you can put the child out of

the house. Now—except in very rare situations—that course of action is unthinkable, but it gives us a starting point, a frame of reference, for thinking about other choices.

To return to the example of Johnny and his parents, a choice for these parents might be that they never go out with their child, although this is only slightly less unthinkable than throwing him out of the house. But let us continue. The parents could put Johnny in charge of the family's eating arrangements for one week. Or they might move out of the house until Johnny is ready to negotiate a truce.

In the realm of more thinkable choices is the idea of giving Johnny a reward of something he wants in return for acceptable dress and grooming. So that the reward will not be in the nature of a bribe, it must be something that would give the parents pleasure too, for instance, a vacation together in some place where the child and the parents want to go.

The choosing is not a one-way street; some choices should involve change on the part of the parents. For example, they might consider the possibility that the world does not find their child as objectionable as they do. They might check with the school and find out that the "aberrant" behavior is something the teachers have come to accept as the norm. They might realize that other parents will be understanding of their frustration and that they really have no need to make excuses.

In any situation that families feel is beyond their capabilities, they also have the choice of getting help from outside the family, from someone who would be able to look at it from an unemotional viewpoint.

There are many more choices open to families; it only

requires that they open their minds and put their imaginations to work to think of them.

Evolving Family Ease

Theoretically, in families where there are basic, agreed-upon guidelines, an issue like the one I have just described between Johnny and his parents could not have come about. When such issues are present, family therapists look for the historical background. How did the situation evolve? How did it get to the point where Johnny is sixteen and looks like a slob and is having daily battles with his parents about it? This is how we start to address the problem, not by trying to solve the immediate situation of how to get the parents through a dinner party (that can only be helped by surgery of some kind—perhaps shipping Johnny off for the night or changing the place of the dinner).

In counseling families on such problems, we would try to decide what evolutionary changes could be made so that the future would be more comfortable for everyone; what agreements could be reached that would take care of the parents' need for structure and social approval as well as the child's need for non-structure and liberation. And we would try to understand what in the family system was keeping them from making this evolution.

Parents cannot change their relationships with their children by trying to handle each fiery situation as it arises. They need to back off if possible and ask themselves what they are doing that they have always done before and how they might do things differently in the future in order to bring about a meaningful change.

For example, Sandra Wolfe uses her father's car when

she goes out at night with her friends. When it is two in the morning and she is still not home—which happens often—her parents become frantic with worry about her. When they say, "I don't want you coming home so late with the car," she answers, "Look, I'm twenty-one years old, I can take care of myself."

The history of the problem here is that it has become a matter of course for this father to lend his grown daughter *his* car under *her* rules.

To change this uncomfortable situation, the parents would have to stop for the moment being parents and just be adult persons lending a car to another adult under certain stipulations. If the parents say, "We're happy to lend you the car, provided you are home by one. These are our rules," then she will have no choice. She will complain and try to get them back into the role of worried parents, but if they hold firm in their position they will start to evolve a new relationship with their daughter.

The crucial part of coming to agreement on anything is that the people involved know what it is they are agreeing to. This isn't as simple as it sounds. Often, when I ask the individual members of a family to tell me what it is they think they have agreed to, they all tell a different story.

To prevent messages from getting garbled, from being heard or said inadequately, family members can actually make a contract, just as if it were a business situation. They can write out a summary of the problem situation and statements by each person involved as to what efforts he or she will make to help solve the problem. They can even sign the agreement to indicate the seriousness of their intent (*not* with the intention of making the agreement legally binding). (An example of a written contract—one concerning chronic indebtedness on the part of a son—is found in chapter 7, "The Social Matrix.")

The contract may seem an extreme measure, but it is really a way by which we can arrive at greater clarity and simplicity in our dealings with each other. Perhaps one or more of the family members may resist the idea of making a contract, and if so, it is probably because they are somewhat afraid of being specific and of having to face the reality of the agreement. When there is a contract in existence, we have no out; we can't later claim that we didn't know what we agreed to.

As in business, a personal contract results from negotiation—the process of give and take. If family members can't agree, it may be necessary to ask someone from outside the family to come in and help the negotiations along. Almost always that person will be able to show the family some aspect of the problem they didn't see themselves. If the family members are adamantly opposed, the outside person may be needed as a "mediator," just as in labor-management stalemates, where someone with no stake in the settlement comes in and says, "Okay, let's give a little on each side and come to some realistic accommodation."

What happens if an agreement is made—whether by contract or not—and one of the parties breaks it? Suppose Sandra made a contract with her parents to be in by a certain hour, but she keeps coming in later than the stipulated time?

When a contract is broken, the family has a new set of circumstances to deal with. They have to renegotiate or find an agreement that seems practical to everyone. First, however, they have to ask themselves why the contract was broken. For example, if Sandra continues to bring the car home late, knowing that she will lose her driving privileges as a result, then we have to consider the possibility that she doesn't wish to have the car, or responsibility for the car, anymore.

This interaction in the Wolfe family is a somewhat simplified example of trying to evolve change in relationships. It says nothing of the pull the past exerts on both the parents and the child to go on behaving toward each other as they always have—the child loading her parents with worry, the parents accepting the burden. But the story illustrates one of the basic steps in evolving ease, which is to speak and react in a different way at the key points in the interchange. "One o'clock, these are our rules" is a very different proposition from "Don't come in so late."

Parents should not be afraid to speak and act differently. I think children are much more pliable, amenable, and capable of change than their elders. They can bear with ground rules, so long as the rules are few and fair and unmistakable in their boundaries. Where there is room for misinterpretation, rules will be misinterpreted.

When you take a clear, unpopular position with your child, it is important to take it freely and be ready to feel some of the "guilties" of not being as "good" a parent as you were before. Your child can live with that approach very well—in all probability, more easily than you can. However, if you do not take a clear position, but instead stand around ruminating and stewing, your child will pick up the angry vibrations and then he will feel guilty and responsible for your condition.

Evolving ease does not necessarily mean doing away completely with dis-ease. It means the integration and the allowance of differences. Even in extreme situations, where there are absolutely polarized differences that seem unresolvable, a well-functioning family will be able to live with the lack of resolution. The differences and dis-ease play a part in establishing the resiliency of the family. Whatever the dispute—let us say it is the dress code—the functioning family can live with it as an issue. When they can't resolve or change it, they allow it to evolve its own resolution. By that I mean, they find a middle way whereby they can meet together, dressed in ways that express their separateness, without being entirely at ease with that expression of separateness. Mother may not like seeing her daughter in carpenter pants, but she doesn't nag about it. She doesn't allow it to become the focus of conversation. And from this her daughter learns that it is possible for people to live together while allowing each other's differences.

Fear of Facing the World

For all the testing of limits that children do, I think the truth of the matter is that no one wishes to be completely emancipated. I believe that children look for and need authority in their lives; they want their parents to be parents. Indeed, most people would probably like a benevolent, all-loving parent around forever.

I'm reminded particularly in this connection of a man I know, a very plainspoken, well-meaning man, who at one stage in his relationship with his college-age son was unsure how he should talk to the young man—whether as his peer or as his father. One day, as the two were walking down the street, they saw a beautiful woman coming toward them and my friend commented in language of the sort more usually heard in Army barracks than in family get-togethers. The boy got furious at hearing his father talk this way. He wanted his father to be as he had always been —someone the boy could look up to. He might have accepted a reference to the woman's looks, but not in the language he himself used with his male peers.

Recently I heard children in a residential school for delinquent boys telling a television interviewer that they welcomed the school's rigorous discipline because it put order in their lives. This reinforced my belief that families must have order and must bring order into their children's lives, and that a primary responsibility of parents is to set parameters so that their adolescent and teenage children do not become frightened by having too much freedom. But the balance—between well-functioning parameters and stifling discipline—is a very delicate one to reach and hold. Often parents misread the message behind their children's early moves toward emancipation. When offspring go away to school and start setting their own limits, they are not claiming total liberation. They're saying, in effect, "I'm away at school, I'm setting my own times, I'm setting my own study habits, I'm setting my own friends, I'm setting my own relationships, I'm setting my own sexual *mores*, I'm setting a lot of things, but don't be confused by what I am doing. I am still your son [or, "I am still your daughter"], and I am still somewhat or very much dependent on you and I don't want that to change. I'm not saying to you that I'm grown. I don't want to be told that I ought to be on my own because I'm an adult in years; I'm not on my own—I'm just somewhat removed from where I was before and I'm testing my wings."

The anxiety of the child about exercising freedom is mirrored by the anxiety of the parents. Sometimes parents allow their children only episodes of freedom and not the continuity of freedom. By freedom I don't mean disconnection from the family or withdrawal of parental authority, but rather a measure of trust which is given and which increases as the child proves capable of exercising judgment and responsibility. Freedom itself can't be given to children; it must evolve. The process is one in which children come with their requests to be allowed to do certain things—or they simply do them—and parents react positively rather than negatively to these moves, seeing them as strivings for independence.

Some parents worry less than others about what their kids do, but this does not mean that they are any less "good" as parents than those who worry more. The tendency to worry about children, I think, has a lot to do with the cultural origins of families. Like other generational patterns, the pattern of overprotection is hard to break. Parents who were allowed latitude to experiment from their early years have an easier time when they see their children trying risky things. The overprotectors will need to face up to certain questions. What precisely are the risks? Can parents, in any case, guarantee the safety and long life of their children? How will children learn if they do nothing that strains their capabilities? Indeed, the more mistakes the children make—and live through—the more they will learn.

Rather than clamping a lid on the child's risky projects, parents should simply stay within the limits of prudence. For example, Jan Fiore went to her parents with plans for backpacking through Europe in the company of two other girls her age (nineteen), intending to pay for the trip with money she had earned working Saturdays in a boutique. Initially her mother was shocked, despite her awareness that for the past twenty years young Americans on summer vacation have been going to Europe in droves. Somehow she was alarmed that her very pretty and demure daughter would soon be one of these unsupervised travelers. Her husband saw the matter differently and discussed it with her when they were alone. "Look," he said, "the likelihood that kids will get killed or hurt or raped while traveling in Europe is probably less than if they stayed here where it happens with cars and booze and drugs. I'm frightened too, but why not let her go?" They talked until they were able to sort out which of her fears were irrational and which were based on fact, and eventually they were able to agree.

Jan—as they told her next day—could go, but there were ground rules and preparations they insisted upon. They asked her to give them an itinerary and set up a loose communication network of addresses where she could pick up mail. They got travel books out of the library and helped her do research on the trip, turning up some useful facts about things she should avoid. They saw to it that whatever dental work she needed done was taken care of and that she went to a doctor for all the necessary immunization shots. They had her travel companions over to the house and reassured themselves that the two young women were not lacking in judgment. They gave her the addresses of relatives in Europe and wrote ahead to say that she might be turning up. They told her to telephone them collect whenever necessary and gave her a bank credit card to use in case of emergency. Finally, they gave the girls a send-off party, took them to the airport, and said good-bye. They were not without misgivings and fears, but they were happy to think that they'd worked as a family to make the trip both safe and fun.

Parents Need Confidence, Too

The transitional years are especially a time when parents and offspring need confidence—confidence of parents to let the transition occur, confidence of children to try their liberating moves.

Children learn confidence by trying, and trying again, regardless of any mistakes or failures they may commit. Parents help build a child's confidence by giving him credit for trying, even if his effort doesn't succeed. To cite a child for failure only undermines confidence. Parents further build a child's confidence by showing trust and allowing their child to take charge of his or her life in ever-increasing ways. When they give a child responsibility it is important to give it entirely, not to hold back part of it; the withheld part may be the crucial part, the real signifier of trust.

Less is written and spoken about parents' need for confidence during this stage of family life. Parents see in themselves the signs of age—the wrinkles, the middle-age spread, the lessening of libidinal drives—and they feel a natural jealousy (which to them seems unnatural) when they look on their maturing offspring. It is not easy for a father to realize that his son has grown into a man taller and more virile than he is, or for a mother to see that she is losing her attractiveness while her daughter is coming into the bloom of youthful beauty.

Unfortunately, the young are often blind to the sense of inadequacy parents feel when they measure their diminishing selves against the untarnished, energetic, crowding presence of their growing children. Perhaps a fitting close to this discussion of the transitional years would be a reminder to the young that confidence is not their problem alone. Their parents need it as much—if not more—than they do.

3

THE SCHOOL EXPERIENCE

Today in the United States the average middle-class twenty-two-year-old has spent almost a lifetime in school. His or her parents have spent thousands of dollars—perhaps as much as fifty thousand dollars—on college alone. In terms of time and money, these are astonishing costs for the privilege of getting an education, yet few families seem to question the validity of this particular American way. Students seek degrees and parents pay for them and yet, very often, the dream of a better life through higher education is never realized.

It may seem that little more could be said on the subject of the school experience, but I have seen many instances where insight into the systemic operation of families has helped students and their parents deal with problems at school and derive greater benefits from the investment of time and money that schooling exacts.

Although college is supposed to be a time of self-motivation and self-limitation for the young person, parents, too, have a role to play in the experience. Usually they pay for it (or most of it); usually they have their home and themselves ready and waiting when the student returns on holidays; and sometimes, if their child is going to school nearby, they are the providers of room and board during the college years. So, although the college student is now largely self-limiting, his or her emancipation is still far from complete.

When Problems Arise at School

Before going to the issues of the college years, there is one aspect of earlier schooling that I feel is sometimes wrongly handled with unfortunate consequences to the student in later years. This is the tendency of parents and teachers to leave children out of the consulting process when problems arise at school. The parents—often it is the mother alone—deal with the school authorities and practice a kind of secrecy where the student himself is concerned.

Let me give you an example. A couple who came to see me had been told by school authorities that their teenage son (a C-plus student) was not really able to meet academic requirements of the prep school he attended and would do well to transfer elsewhere. The boy knew nothing of this and the parents believed it would be hurtful for him to know, so they decided to comply with the school's request, giving their son another reason for the planned change.

I convinced the parents instead to tell their son what the school was saying and to meet *as a family* with the school authorities to discuss the problem. I pointed out that the secrecy they were practicing in an attempt to protect their son could prove far more undermining and detrimental than the proposed lowering of his academic goals.

The need for this move was based on my belief that systems function best when members are honest and open about their needs. To practice secrecy is to cover up our needs. It might be compared to the well-intentioned efforts of humans when they try to manipulate ecological systems in nature: the good they do to one part of the system often tends to have harmful effects on the system as a whole.

My point about schools and parents is this: whenever a problem comes up that calls for parental involvement, the response should be systemic. Any meeting on the matter should include the father, the mother, and the child—and siblings too, if that is possible. Whenever students are failing exams, cutting classes, acting out, it is not merely a school problem but a *family-and-school* problem, and the school and the family should unite and deal with it together.

Family Planning for College

Obviously the very act of starting college does not mean that a marked change has come over the young person who only a few months before was in high school. As we have said, the transition from adolescence to maturity is a gradual and a highly individual process. It occurs early for some and later for others, and, unfortunately, there are those for whom the transition never occurs. Thus, while we have labeled our subject here "the college years," much of what follows applies as well to students in their later teens who are living away from home.

Where did the assumption come from that college should immediately succeed high school in the normal course of events? Perhaps it was a logical extension of compulsory education for all Americans through grade school. In any case, it is now rather rare to find a family in which the children choose not to go to college despite having the wherewithal to do so. (My own family is one of the few I know who fit into that category. Higher education was preached but the norm called for the sons to go into business without the benefit of a college degree.)

I raise this point because I feel that parents and their college-age children do not generally consult as they might on the children's actual readiness and desire for the college experience. Some young people go to college simply because that is what their friends do; they are not primarily interested in an education. And that's okay for those parents who don't have to mortgage their lives in order to send their children to college.

For some, the choice of a school is especially important; for example, it can be hard on those students who need individual attention if they end up in schools where almost nobody gets individual attention. Some students become disillusioned by the emphasis on getting a degree—the "paper chase," as they call it—particularly if they had looked forward to college as a time for new and varied and stretching experiences.

Establishing a student's desire and readiness for college is a fairly simple matter; getting him there is something else. Many parents today are in the position of a friend of mine who told me sadly that it would soon be time to send his daughter to college and that there was no way he could do it; he simply didn't have that kind of money over and above his other obligations.

For some time now, the college experience has generally been within the reach of middle-class American families, but what of the future? According to a recent projection, it will cost the graduates of 1990 about ninety thousand dollars to get a degree at a major institution. This suggests to me that college will either have to become free—or relatively free—in the United States, or that it will go out of business entirely except for the children of the very rich (which would put higher education back to where it began in this country).

Today most families have to stretch to meet the expenses of college. Whatever way they do it—a long-term loan, a lower standard of living, other plans or projects canceled—the effort is a stress on the family. And the stress is all the greater if parents don't involve the college-bound child in the effort. This is something parents are often reluctant to do; they handle the problem, but they don't handle it openly enough where the student is concerned.

Certainly a young person who is old enough to go to college is old enough to share in the financial realities of the college experience, and his parents should be willing to burden him with those realities. The sooner parents bring their children into the planning, the less of a problem college will be. The joint effort can begin when the child is entering the early teens. There should be family discussions of the possible ways of financing college. Perhaps out of the family income a certain amount could be put every month into a tuition fund; perhaps during high school the child could work toward admission to certain colleges that offer scholarships or other assistance; or the student might plan on getting an education in a state or city university system, if that is what the family can afford. These are but a few of the many ways a family can begin well ahead of time to work together on meeting the financial demands of college.

If parents take the entire financial burden on themselves with the idea of protecting the child from the problem, the effect on the family can be damaging in many ways. The added stress on the parents will make itself felt in all areas of family life. Moreover, if a family exhausts its resources putting one child through college, a younger child may be denied the opportunity and be angry because of this inequity. The student, too, is affected if he feels he is benefiting from his family's sacrifices. The pressure on him may be so powerful that his evolution to adulthood will be defined more by the family's expectations than by his own maturational needs.

A child's willingness to leave home for school, coupled with his parents' ability to turn responsibility over to him and to live without his presence in the house, is an indicator of the family's evolutionary process.

A Long Step Toward Independence

That September morn when a child sets off to begin college is always momentous in family life. A new chapter begins in which the young person takes on almost complete responsibility for himself. His willingness to do this, coupled with his parents' willingness to turn responsibility over to him, is a crucial indicator of the evolutionary process in their family.

Whether the student lives at home or away, it is important that parents keep very loose reins on him during the college years. It is a time when family relationships need to change, and change cannot come about unless there is plenty of breathing and moving space in the parent-child relationship. But simply "letting go" is not the answer. The student himself may be fearful when he sees the distance widening between himself and his home, and he may try to resist the process. For example, if a child is not ready for the degree of independence that is thrust on him when he goes away to school for the first time, he may put pressure on his parents to "rein him in." He may do this by calling home frequently, coming home at every opportunity, asking for a bigger allowance, failing some courses, and so forth. Parents need to see these moves for what they are—expressions of the child's lonesomeness and worry—and not overrespond by trying to reestablish their previous closeness with their child.

When a child begins college, he also begins to exclude his family as a pervasive influence in his life and to open himself to an array of experiences and freedoms and work pressures that will greatly widen the distance between himself and his parents. If the child is living away rather than at home, his parents have to accept that henceforth they will be more or less ignorant of their child's day-to-day activities—of his friends, his study habits, his forms of experimentation, and the like; there is no way they can know what he's doing unless he chooses to tell them (and, in fact, they're probably better off not knowing).

The exclusionary process generally is easier if the young person lives away at school (assuming he is really ready for college) than if he lives at home while attending college. He will be more available to the total educational and social experience, which has as much to do with the exercise of freedom as it does with study and research and class attendance.

But many young people don't go away to college; they go to local schools and continue to live at home during the college years. It takes even greater skill and understanding on the part of the parents to let their relationship with their child undergo real change at this time, to let themselves be excluded more and more from his activities while he continues to live under their roof. If they want him to gain as much as possible from college, they have to build new freedoms into the home atmosphere. In practical terms this means not making an issue of it if the child doesn't show up as expected, not questioning him as to who or what kept him out late, not minding if he is still up studying at 2 A.M., and so forth.

The Widmers came to see me partly because they were having trouble adjusting to this change. Their son Joe had gone away to college when he was seventeen and a half, and although he seemed to be liking it, his grades for the first semester were barely passing. In the second semester he failed most of his subjects and was told by the school authorities that he could continue his studies there only if he maintained a B-minus average.

Joe's parents thought it would be better if he went to a school in New York City, where they lived. He wasn't ready to be on his own, they said, and his performance in his first year away at college was proof of this. After arguing with them (somewhat less vehemently than he usually argued), Joe agreed to the plan. He was accepted by a college in Manhattan and he returned to school there the next September. He did relatively well, but his living home as a student raised many problems with the family.

Joe's parents were concerned, first of all, about his study habits. They wanted him to put in several hours of study every weekday night and to be in by eleven o'clock any time he went out. Joe objected; he wanted to set his own study habits and hours. The difference of views developed into a serious battle and was one of the reasons his family came to see me.

The formula I worked out with the Widmers caused grumbling on both sides (as fair settlements usually do), but Joe and his parents accepted it. It required him to be in by eleven o'clock Monday through Thursday (Joe groaned about this). On the other hand, he would set his own hours of study (his parents were skeptical about this). If he did well during the first term—"well" being defined as a B average—he would have greater freedom in the matter of coming and going.

For a family to change its norms at all is difficult; to change them on a given day in order to harmonize with the life-style of a college student is superdifficult. Each family has its unique set of circumstances to be considered in trying to reach an accommodation. Joe, for example, was signaling by his failure that he wasn't ready to leave home and perhaps also that he doubted whether home was ready to be without him. The truth was that his parents were having marital troubles and that his younger brother was causing them worry with certain behavioral problems. Although Joe couldn't have articulated his feelings, he really felt needed at home.

When I told this family my assessment of their problem —that Joe's failing in school was a positive response to a family need—they all looked at me askance. Nevertheless, as the year progressed and as the conflicts between the generations in this household were eased, Joe started doing better at school. He even got a part-time job, which lessened the financial strain on his parents. In the following year, his parents worked hard to improve their relationship, and when Joe saw them sincerely trying to save their marriage, he showed less need to be involved in family life and instead enlarged his relationships with his peers and others outside the family.

It may be difficult for parents to appreciate—unless they are able to harken back to their own college days—how difficult it can be for some students to make the change from high school to college. Besides having to carry a heavier work load, college freshmen have to establish their identities with a whole new group of peers. The student who excelled scholastically in high school and who gets into a top college as a result finds herself no longer exceptional but just one of a class full of brains. The star football player who gets an athletic scholarship may be only one of a dozen All-State, All-Star freshman prodigies competing for first-string quarterback. Some students thrive on the expanded atmosphere and handle it well from the beginning. On the other end of the spectrum are those students for whom the freedom and responsibility of campus life are a tremendous stress. Many of these students fail; some break down psychologically; an increasing number commit suicide. As long as our system of higher education functions as it does, with the strong emphasis on competitive scoring, we will have anxious and despairing students. It behooves us all to work on this problem and see if we can evolve a less pressured system.

The Case for Boarding Schools

I think there is a case to be made for boarding school as a helpful step in the process of emotional growth and separation. In some families, boarding school is a tradition that has come to fit in with the family's style of operation. But in other families, where there is the financial ability but not the tradition of sending a child to boarding school, the idea may be approached with feelings of guilt.

To decide if boarding school is the right move for the child, a family should establish whether it fits in with his or her needs as well as the family's needs. A child who is maturing at a faster rate may be comfortable with an earlier separation from family, whereas a slow developer may not. If the parents also are comfortable with the move, the next step is for the family to decide together on the school that seems most suitable on all points—its scholastic emphasis, its distance from home, and so forth. Once the choice is made to everyone's satisfaction, the parents can dispense with any idea that they are "packing the child off." In fact, they are giving the child an experience that will help him in his progress toward emancipation.

Vacation Times

Vacations from school aren't always the carefree times the word connotes. When the student who has been enjoying the freedoms of college life comes home to a household where the old rules still apply, an adjustment has to be made by both generations. When Johnny asks for a bourbon and soda, whereas before he always drank beer; when Sally asks to bring home her lover—whose wishes are to be respected, the parents' or the child's?

As we have said, this is a time when limits are being tested, and testing is a necessary part of the growth process. Unfortunately for us parents, I believe it is *we*, rather than our children, who have to make most of the adjustments in this situation. We need to loosen our rules sufficiently so that the child will not feel a radical change when he leaves the college atmosphere and reenters the home atmosphere. If the transition is too hard to make, the parents and their child will get into conflict over the child's new norms. It is important to try to avoid these conflicts; if there are differences, they should be handled with a side-by-side rather than a confrontational attitude, as we described in the previous chapter.

It shouldn't be forgotten that parents undergo life

changes of their own at the time their children are coming
to adulthood in the college scene. Especially if there are no
younger children at home, it is a time when parents will be
trying to restructure their relationship with each other.
They should not feel duty-bound to welcome their child
home from school any time the child wants to come.
There may be weekends or holidays when they would really prefer to have the house to themselves, and when this
happens, they should be able to say to their child, for example, "Just now we're getting used to the new atmosphere here at home with you away, and we think it would
be good for us to be alone this weekend. We love you, and
we know what it feels like to be lonesome, but please try to
deal with your lonesomeness for a little while and come
home later when we'll all be more comfortable together."

A statement like this is not easy to make. It goes against
that ingrained belief that "good parents" should want their
child home. To be workable, it has to reflect the feelings of
both parents; they have to be clear with each other as to
whether or not they want the child home at that time.
Also, such a statement should not come out of the blue. If
a family is very close in its relationships, a sudden refusal
will come as a hurtful rejection. Language, too, is important. If the parents need to be alone, they should put that
message to their child in terms that express their continuing love for him and the pleasure it will give them to see
him when the time is right.

The need for parents and children to have a "rest" from
each other is probably greatest at the time the child first
goes away to college. The freshman who has been away for
only a few weeks may worry about whether or not to go
home, while his parents are concerned about whether or
not they should visit him. Usually it is better for the process of family growth if parents and child can get through

the early anxiety without closing the physical distance that has abruptly opened between them.

A final comment on the subject of vacations. It is very common, particularly in these days of soaring college costs, for young people to work during their summer vacations. Some, however, will join their families on vacation trips or activities, just as they did when they were younger. The point I wish to make is that these young adults cannot be expected to go along with plans unquestioningly as they did when they were small. They deserve a larger voice in the selection and planning of a family vacation. It's their right, and it will help ensure a successful vacation for everyone.

How Parents Can Help—and Hinder

Beyond financing college, how far should parents involve themselves in their children's college careers?

Here, again, it may take a change in viewpoint for parents to stop being the controllers of their children's schooling. Remember, parents start controlling early in their children's lives by the very act of forcing them to attend school. The child doesn't make that decision; society makes it for him.

Certain aspects of compulsory schooling are desirable. Society needs order and needs educated people. But the forcing of education on children tends to lessen independent thought and feelings of independence. (Perhaps we are seeing the effects of this today in the seeming inability of leaders in government and industry to break from outmoded ways and find new inventive solutions to problems in manufacturing, transportation, utilities, delivery of health care, and so forth.)

Although parents may not actually force a field of endeavor on a child, rarely do they say to him, "The world is open to you." They tend to have their own biases that they may transmit by their choice of schools—and thus of available curricula—so that the possibilities for the child open in certain directions and not in others. We can only wonder how much creativity never comes to flower because of these educational biases.

Sometimes parents try to push their children into courses of study for which the children have no enthusiasm. This I think can have only negative results. In the short term, such students are more likely to drop out or do mediocre work; in the long term, they are more likely to experience career problems and discontent in their later life.

Probably the most powerful positive influence parents can have on their children's fields of study is through example. A child who looks up to a parent who is a doctor or lawyer or scientist or scholar or musician or businessman (or businesswoman) may well choose to follow in his parent's footsteps. The difference here is that the child is following a family norm, not succumbing to family pressure.

There are parents who put pressure on their children to score straight A's. I'm reminded of a mother I met at a college graduation who said in front of her son (his thesis had been graded A-minus), "Can you imagine? He didn't make honors! He could have done better." Though others within hearing of this comment were shocked, it obviously came as no surprise to the young man; he had been listening to this kind of thing all his life. Here he was, graduating in the higher ranks of his class, yet there was little joy for him in the event. He seemed almost visibly weighed down by his mother's criticism.

Parents can apply pressure on their children to excel, but

not in the way of the mother I have just described. Young people need to feel the subjects they are studying, the projects they are working on, are part of the real world, not something designed by educators as ways of torturing them. Parents can help by being a kind of bridge to reality for their children. They can show a serious interest in the subjects and projects, and they can express their pleasure when the student does well, even if only passably well.

With this attitude to encourage them, students are more likely to enjoy their work and do it better. If, on the contrary, they are only working to satisfy parents who care only about the bottom line—the final grade—they are in danger of becoming the "class grinds," anxious, depressed loners—which is an awful price to pay for academic honors.

It's usual these days for colleges to inquire where they should send the marks of newly enrolled students: to the parents or to the students, or to both at the same time.

With the good intention of helping their child grow up, some parents answer that they prefer the marks to go directly to the student. Are they doing the right thing?

There is, of course, no right or wrong in this matter. I feel, however, that parents who are sending a child through college or graduate school have a right to know how well that child is doing. Even though the student is now largely self-limiting and self-motivated, he is still dependent on his parents financially and is not really out of the home. Parents who make the emancipating gesture of having the marks sent to the student only will almost certainly feel left out of the educational process.

In summary, then, I would say it is poor policy for parents to be too controlling of their children's education. They want the best for their child, and they may believe they know what is best, but there is no way they can any longer implant interest or abilities in their child. Ideally, their role is to open the world with its myriad possibilities for their child and to help him, insofar as they are able, to develop in directions that are congenial with his temperament and inborn faculties.

Dropping Out

When Phil—who was twenty-two and had three months to go before getting his degree—called his parents to say that he was quitting school, there wasn't much they could do about it—except cry. They reasoned and they argued with him, but they couldn't sway his decision. (None of their arguments, however, took into account that they were on the verge of divorce and that one of the things that dropping out would do for Phil was to spare him the pain of a family reunion at his graduation.)

Dropping out can come early or it can come late; some students walk away from school in the week of their final exams. And rarely are they able to make their parents understand the reasons why.

Whatever the reasons in any particular case, each and every child who walks away from school is making a clear statement: "I cannot now go on." Perhaps that child needs time and space, perhaps he is not mature enough to take responsibility for himself, perhaps he can't keep up with the work, perhaps he can't stand the pressure of deadlines and competition, perhaps he feels the need to change what he believes is a wrong direction in his life. There are students who drop out precisely because they love school. For fifteen, sixteen, or seventeen years they have been studying; they are comfortable with that life and they wonder what will happen to them when suddenly they are "graduated"

—pushed out into a world where they will have to be something other than students. By not graduating, they avoid having to take this important step in their life cycle. They don't solve anything by this move, but it gives them time to examine their choices.

When kids drop out, their parents should first of all realize that the child can pick up on college at any later time in life; that, in fact, students who return in later years usually get much more out of the experience of higher education.

Furthermore, although a college degree is usually a requisite for entering most high-income fields, it is not necessarily true that kids who get better jobs out of better colleges are also happier kids, or that they lead fuller lives or make better marriages. I understand the real and appropriate anxiety of parents about how their drop-out is going to live and support himself. But it is almost impossible for a young person of twenty-one or so to make a really wrong choice. The choice, whatever it is, is just a single step in his progress through life.

The least helpful thing parents can do is make the dropping-out a matter of conflict. If they do this, then the child's moves to save himself from an intolerable stress merely land him in another stressful (and perhaps even less tolerable) situation. Instead of being confrontational, parents should try a side-by-side discussion of the problem with their child, asking him how he feels, what he thinks he would like to do next, how he thinks they can help him.

The parents may be tempted to put him right back where he was, or to start him as soon as possible in another school. Unless the child really wants this, the second go-around is not likely to be any more successful than the first. By forcing or persuading him to return to school, the parents deprive him of a crucial element in the educational process—the assumption of responsibility for his own life.

Student Sabbaticals

A kind of evolutionary change has been going on in the long-accepted idea that our children should finish high school, then go on to college, and after that start right in working for a living. The kids themselves have been the leaders in this change. They began taking time off and their parents called it dropping out. Then it became clear that what they were doing was something different, that the term "dropping out" was not appropriate to describe the process. Instead we began to speak of students "taking sabbaticals," something similar to the year a college professor takes off after every six years of teaching—time during which he or she is supposed to study, work on new projects, and broaden interests.

Now society is coming to see that a sabbatical can be a positive experience for a young person. The student's time off can be a time for travel, employment, or even—dare I say it—goofing off after going to school for most of his life. Most of all, the sabbatical is a time for students to integrate some of the realities of life that they are just beginning to recognize and question.

Many colleges and universities now encourage student sabbaticals. They keep the administrative red tape to a minimum and give the students special recognition when they return to school afterward.

For the families, however, it may not be easy to view the sabbatical as a positive move, especially if the student stays home during his time off. Parents who have probably just gotten used to the child being away have to accept a young adult living with them who may appear to the outside world—and maybe even to them—to be living a lethargic, unproductive, unprofitable existence.

One of the questions they are faced with, of course, is whether or not to continue to support the child during the sabbatical as they would if he or she were still in school.

I think this is a question that can be allowed to solve itself. By that I mean, the family should do whatever is in keeping with its own way of operating. If money is a problem, and the child and family have had to stretch their resources in order to pay for college, then the student should do something to earn money while taking the extended time off. In circumstances like these, if the child wants to travel, he might say to his parents, "I'm going away and I've provided for most of the expense but I need a little help from you each month." In a household where money is not a problem, the family might appropriately provide all the necessary funds for a child's period of travel; the money would be freely offered and freely accepted.

The family that has been maturing and changing its spatial relationships can make this kind of transaction simply. They are able to treat the sabbatical not as an aberration but as a positive move toward emancipation. And in truth, perhaps no other time in life will do so much to build the ego of the young person, or provide so much in the way of creative experience and sheer adventure.

4

THE NEW ADULTS

The graduation dinner had been one of almost frenetic gaiety, but now as the families lingered over coffee, the mood grew pensive. Earlier that day the graduates had been elated because the grind of college was finally over. Their parents had been happy for them and relieved, too, to see that their own responsibilities had been fulfilled. Now the many drinks consumed were having their full effect and the gaiety was giving way to sadness. Parents and offspring alike were seeing a new stage of life opening before them. For the young the time had come to go into the world and see what that unknown territory held for them. For their parents the time had come to surrender all control over their children—and with it much of their power to help them. For some of those parents the time had come to face the issues of their future aloneness.

The combined ways that young people have of claiming their adulthood—physical growth, self-determination, geographical separation from their parents, involvement with persons, work, and interests outside the purview of the home—all this has a heavy impact on the life of the family system, and rarely do any of these changes occur without conflict.

Just consider, for example, the ambivalent feelings of

parents as their children are making these moves. They want them to mature and go out on their own, but they are afraid of being lonely without them. In the back of their minds, they look forward to the children being out so they can have some peace and quiet, and at the same time they feel guilty about having those expectations. The financial strain of the college years is almost preferable to the sense of vacancy they feel after the children move out. They may look at each other and say, "What are we going to do rattling around in all these empty rooms?"

So the time of the new adults is a time of highly confused feelings. We humans are not like the birds: they seem to know exactly when their young are ready to fly, and when the fledglings are gone, the parents proceed to raise yet another brood. We, on the contrary, have a very complex system of inputs. Our separation moves have to occur in a sequence that allows family relationships to be resolved and put at ease, otherwise our future relationships will be complicated by that lack of resolution.

Jobs, Careers, and Other Life Decisions

Separation is the most difficult phase of family life. During this time the distance between parents and children, which was practically nonexistent at the time of the child's birth, widens to a critical point, neither so large that the generations feel cut off from each other, nor so narrow that it restricts the development of the young person. At the same time the levels of authority the parents and children occupy in relation to each other are also changing. And because of the complicated geometry of families (the many possible ways that members of a family stand in relation to each other), the chances for error are great, so great that

perfection in family life is beyond the reach of even the
most skilled of us.

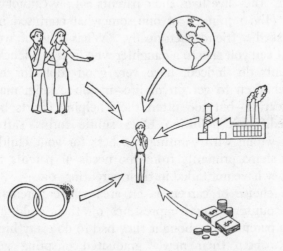

*Separation is a very difficult phase of family life. Questions
of love, work, money, and the world "out there" confront the
new adults. Parents want to help, but they're not sure how to
do it.*

I am speaking basically about the expectations of parents during the time of separation: about what they want
for their children; why they want those things; why their
attempts to be helpful so often seem to miscarry. A
woman I know voiced the common plaint of parents at
this time when their children are separating: "How do I
help them find what they want to do with their lives? How
do I guide them in their life decisions?"

It seems to be characteristic of parents everywhere that
they want to see their grown children make decisions,
build careers, accumulate money, show steady progress,
and somehow achieve more than they themselves have
achieved. They think that if they try hard enough some-

how magically their children will "do better." What often happens, however, is that their children seem to do "worse," they live lives their parents simply cannot understand. (I'm reminded of one somewhat confused mother who asked a friend rhetorically, "What kind of wedding present can you give to a daughter who lives in a truck?")

Parents do, indeed, have very good tools for helping their children to get on in life—in job-seeking, marriage, child-rearing—but too often their helping efforts become polluted. This pollution takes subtle forms (after all, what's wrong with wanting the best for your children?), and it stems primarily from the needs of parents to feel that they have not failed in their parenting role.

The choice of careers is an area where parents often apply counterproductive pressures on their children. I've known parents who thought they had to do everything possible to help their newly graduated offspring get the "right" job, no matter how much time and effort it took. In these families there seems to be a fear operating that if the young person makes a mistake that mistake will haunt him or her for a lifetime.

There is nothing less promising, to my way of thinking, than the graduate who has "made up his mind" on a job or career that will occupy him for the rest of his life in a narrow range of activity. Yet haven't we all heard parents say that their kids should decide what they want to be before they get out of college? These parents forget that life has many avenues and a whole spectrum of colors, and that one of the ways we might avoid dying of boredom at fifty or fifty-five is to try different things while we are young and find out then some of the possibilities life holds.

Like life itself, a career tends to be a succession of ups and downs. The ups are generally rewarded with progressively higher dollar amounts as well as higher levels of satisfaction and responsibility. Everyone's first job ought to be a low-level job in something totally unconnected with their own family. (The young person who goes straight into a family business will never know what it means to be strictly an employee of others.) The first job might be a service job at a low wage. Now, although a job like this might be the norm in some families, in middle- and upper-income families it sometimes causes a storm when a child takes such work. I listened to a mother and father bemoaning the fact that their son's job as a waiter had made it impossible for him to be with them for Christmas dinner. In reality, this job was one of the first independent moves the boy had made. I think also, in this connection, of a young woman, Lisa, who has her parents climbing the walls, as she puts it, in their disappointment in her progress. After graduating with honors from a major university, she went to work in a bookstore for eighty-five dollars a week: subsequently she married, separated, and went back to school to take a counseling degree. Now, at twenty-nine, she is single again and starting her first job as a counselor. Her parents think she has been squandering her talents; Lisa, on the contrary, believes that her twenties have been a progression of mature decisions, her own way of evolving her individuality.

In some families, the children's attitude toward work is adversely influenced when they see their parents making work an end in itself, a time occupier, a substitute for a fulfilling family life. And the more space and time the work takes up, the less fulfilling the family life becomes. Good times don't generally happen spontaneously in families like these; they have to be scheduled, like everything else. The child who picks up this pattern may grow up to be a workaholic just like his or her parent(s).

There is no question, then, that parents can and do influence their children in these matters. The question is, How can they be the helpful influence they want so much to be?

Questions of Success and Failure

Once again we come to the question, What can parents do? How can they offer guidance to the new adults? How can they help them without being counterproductive in those very efforts to help? What expectations are realistic, which ones are merely invitations to disillusion?

It is the norm for parents to want to see their children succeed in whatever terms they—the parents—equate with success, whether it be happiness, health, riches, high repute, or whatever. Some parents look upon themselves as successful; others see themselves as failures. But regardless of whether they have succeeded or failed themselves, they tend to judge the success of their children according to their *own* standards—as if their own standards automatically applied to their children.

What is success, after all? What is failure? Who can judge? Which is more important, that a child's life-style be pleasing to his parents, or that it satisfy the needs of the child? In this matter of parental ambition, I could probably cite no clearer case than that of Nicky, a young woman whose doctor father still disapproves of her career choice, even though she did brilliantly in obtaining her law degree and subsequently passed the New York Bar exam on the first try at the age of twenty-six. In her father's eyes Nicky will not succeed until she becomes—like him—a doctor.

It cannot be emphasized too much that for different people maturity arrives at different times and in ways that are not easily identifiable. Children go forward by trying new things, failing in things, succeeding in things, trying, failing, succeeding—and all these things come together in the individual at an age that cannot be predicted.

Children must experience failure at some time in their lives, otherwise they will have nothing against which to measure their successes. The right choices they make today are based on the wrong choices they made in the past—in matters of money, school, love, sex, friendship, and all the other areas of life. All the behaviors a child exhibits can be used as the basis for positive learning, *provided* the parents understand this and do not label the doer and the behavior as "failing," "inept," "incapable," or any of the other losing terms parents tend to attach when they don't see their children rising steadily to the pinnacle of the world.

This may sound like heresy, but an important part of the role of parents is to allow—perhaps even to encourage —their children to make mistakes. When a child makes mistakes, he should be rewarded rather than punished, so that he will not be afraid to try new things in the future. The young man whose job as a waiter kept him from being with his family on Christmas day ought to have been rewarded for his willingness to work. Instead, what he heard from his parents was, "You're wasting your time. You're learning nothing that can help you later on. You couldn't even have dinner with us!"

Parents who enjoy a measure of success often try to smooth the way for their children. If there is an obstacle in their child's path they feel responsible for removing it. A man I know comes to mind in this connection. He studied interior design and architecture, but he came on the job market at a time when opportunities in that field were scarce. Without consulting him, his father got him a job as a bond salesman in a reputable brokerage house. Being a "good" son, he took the job but he hated the work and did it so badly that he was eventually fired. Then the girl he loved called off their engagement. He started drinking heavily then, and for the rest of his life he remained alone and alcoholic, supporting himself by doing odd jobs in the field where his talents lay.

The lack of consultation, the assumption that he knew what was best for his son, doomed this father's helping gesture. Whenever parents run interference for their grown children—as in this example—they leave them no opportunity to come up against the difficult truths of life and to find their own way around the obstacles.

There is a very fine line in the matter of helping kids get jobs. It is most helpful and desirable for parents to use their connections, their experience, and their counsel in this matter. If they say, for example, "Sam Johnson says his company is looking for summer replacements. Why not call him?" they are giving the child information and allowing him or her to use that information. The minute they go beyond this line and start, in effect, to drag the child toward the goal ("I told Sam Johnson he could expect a call from you tomorrow morning"), then the helping is less helpful.

Another example of a well-meaning but misguided parent is the one who says, in effect, "I didn't make it but I'll do my best to see that you do!" The flaw in statements like this is the tone of resignation they carry. Parents who say to themselves, "I've failed, and therefore I am a failure" are giving a message to their child that he or she, too, will be stymied in life. Children think of themselves in many respects as reflections of their parents, and when they fail it is likely to be in some area of life where their parents also failed. "Mom and Dad couldn't do it, so it probably can't be done," seems to be the underlying belief that keeps them from succeeding.

If parents feel disappointed in life or believe themselves to be failures, and if they convey this belief to their children, they cannot realistically expect to help their children break the generational pattern, however much they exhort them to succeed or however well they equip them with the tools of success.

The most helpful thing they can do is to demonstrate to their children that they themselves are capable *at any point in their lives* of changing, of adding to their experience, of doing things differently from before. Even if they try to conceal the darker side of their lives—the fears and imperfections and shortcomings we all have in some measure—their children will see through to the truth. Our power to shape our children's lives lies in the power we have to shape our own lives and in so doing to be role models for them (not necessarily images of perfection).

Resisting the Pull to Come Back

One of the very delicate moments in the emancipation process occurs whenever a new adult recoils from his or her new-found freedom. At such times the parents feel impelled to make supportive moves, first, in order to spare themselves the anxiety they feel over their children's mistakes, and second, in order to reestablish the previous dependent relationship, which they know and are better able to handle. Let me give you an example.

The daughter of a couple I know called them frequently on the phone and talked mainly about her new job with a textile manufacturer. Although she was enthusiastic while at work, when she talked to her parents it was to tell them how hard she was working, how little time she had for fun, how little money she was making in comparison to what she was giving of herself. One weekend when she came to see them, her father told her he thought she should leave the job. He'd back her up financially, buy her a ticket for a Caribbean vacation, do anything she needed to get her out of a painful situation.

Fortunately the girl did not accept. What she really was asking of her parents was that they be friends and commiserate with her and also hear the message implicit in what she was saying—that she was performing well in a very demanding job. The father misheard this message. He fell into the trap of being a problem-solver and responded as he would have done for a very young child in real trouble, by trying to come to her rescue. Had she accepted this kind of help, it would have been regressive both for the parents and the child, a setback to their freedom from the burden of parenthood and to her freedom from childhood dependency.

In these situations it is important for parents not to make the kind of supportive moves that are really unsupportive, not to try to do what they cannot do or to be what they cannot be. Before they do anything, they should remind themselves that emancipation is not a flow, but rather a trial-and-error process, and that their role is to ebb and flow in harmony with the child's uncertain moves toward independence.

Can parents help in any concrete way? Most certainly. I am thinking of a father who helped his son locate the kind of managerial advice he needed in starting a solar-energy business; and another father who went over his daughter's apartment lease with her, making suggestions, but restraining his desire to offer her added money so that she could live in a larger apartment; of the parents who helped their son financially through the first few struggling years of a serious acting career; of a mother who made her daughter comfortable at home during the months she was out of work recuperating from a painful automobile injury. None of these supportive moves had strings attached. They left the new adults free to make their next moves; they respected the efforts the new adults were making to live their own lives and meet their own needs.

How to Deal with Parental Anxiety

However much parents may rationalize, they will always want to alleviate any misfortune or unhappiness that comes to their children. (At least, I have always found this to be true in my own life. And although I question whether this is perhaps a culturally variable trait, I have seen it to be true in families of many different cultural backgrounds.) It is hard for us parents to accept that we cannot be the guarantors of our children's happiness. We watch their struggles from a viewpoint which they, being young, cannot possibly share. Looking back at all the things that have happened to us, we have perspective on what the real issues are. Often, when we see our kids worrying, we know their problem is something very transitory, but we cannot try to push our viewpoint on them. For them it is a *real* worry and we have to let them worry until they come out on the other side of the problem.

How, then, do we deal with our anxieties, aside from getting an ulcer or having a heart attack? (I am not being facetious. People tend to somatize their anxieties—to wear them, in a sense, as physical symptoms that are observable by the outside world.) Our anxiety is real and appropriate, and the physical manifestations—if they don't kill us—are helpful indicators of our need to change the way we deal with our anxieties.

I would like to suggest this approach to controlling parental anxieties at the time of separation. It might be summarized in a three-part formula: admission, sharing, self-assessment.

Admitting our anxiety is the first step in controlling it, yet we cannot easily do this. We are experts, most of us, at burying our anxiety, at saying we do not have it. If someone tells us we are anxious, that only makes us more anxious, so we block out the information. We have to learn to let our anxiety flow, and when it does, we have to be willing to admit what is happening.

The next important step in controlling parental anxiety is to share it. This means talking about the problem with others who are involved, expressing the feelings, the worries, the frights, agreeing on whatever steps can be taken to alleviate the anxiety without infringing on the freedom of the young person who seems to be the cause of the anxiety. (A good example of this kind of sharing is found in chapter 2, in the ground rules agreed on by the girl who wanted to travel and the parents who were anxious for her safety.)

The third step in dealing with parental anxiety is to ask ourselves how much we really have it in our power to change things. The sense of having to be the "strong one," the ever-supportive one, certainly is part of the parental role when our offspring are small and relatively powerless. But this is not a realistic self-image to carry over into a relationship with a grown child. At this point the child should take on the burden and responsibility for his or her own life; that is the whole point of the process of emancipation. We, as parents, are simply not able to protect them or to live life for them.

The following story, which I heard from an old friend, seems to sum up much of what I feel about parenting the new adults. His daughter stopped by his apartment one day and began describing the many problems that beset her in her personal life. As she spoke, he felt his shoulders sagging under the weight of her troubles, and his mind raced to think of solutions that would ease her pain. The more she loaded him down with her problems, the more frustrated and angry he became. Finally, in his exasperation, he blurted out, "There's nothing I can do! I don't know how to solve your problems, I don't know what advice to give you." To this she said quickly, "I don't want your advice, I don't want you to ease my pain. All I want you to do is be here and listen, and let me cry on your shoulder when I need to. That's what you're supposed to do." She said this so convincingly that the weight fell away from him. From that moment on he could listen to her without thinking that he had to come up with solutions, simply with the realization that she trusted him and expected him to do nothing more than give her a loving and sympathetic hearing.

The directness and clarity of the interchange helped that parent understand in a moment what some parents seem never to understand: that with our grown children, the measure of how well we're doing is more in the *lack* of parenting than in any active role we may take. As parents of adults we need to let go of responsibility toward our children and let them find their own path instead. Whereas before we were responsible for *doing,* now we are responsible for *being.* Whereas before we were providers and advisers, now we can be storytellers and fountains of experience. We can and should be available to listen and to give advice when asked—but only when asked. Whether what we know out of our experience is true or false is not the point. The point is that we share what we know with our children. That, I believe, is the magic we can give to them once they are grown.

5

LOVE, SEX, AND MARRIAGE: THE SYSTEM EXPANDS

Ronnie is fifteen and in love. Almost every day he brings his girl friend Sandy home and they sit for hours in his locked room listening to music and talking—sometimes even doing a little homework.

In the beginning Ronnie's parents were amused, but now they're deeply irritated by this behavior. Ronnie and Sandy, they say, are spending too much time together. Yes, they want him to bring his friends home, but with Sandy it has gotten to the point where she is practically living with them, and they feel that it's impinging on their home life and their privacy.

Like parents everywhere, Ronnie's are struggling with the appropriate limitations to place on young love. They know that their children need to fall in love and have close and intimate relationships as preparation for satisfying partnerships in marriage and family, yet they worry about where the early love relationships will lead. They are searching for parameters that will guard their children's welfare while giving them the measure of freedom they need to relate emotionally to others.

Ronnie's parents, for example, might be tempted to clamp down hard on his relationship, to say, "We don't want you having Sandy here that much because you're never available to us and you're doing poorly in school. And, what's more, we don't want you going out all the time with Sandy either, because we don't want you out of the house that much." A reaction like this would put all parties in a bind. Ronnie would have to choose between his family and his love—an impossible choice—and his parents would destroy the possibility of comfortable companionship with their child. Their fighting over the issue could eventually become their only way of communicating.

What, then, might Ronnie's parents say in this situation? Perhaps something like this: "Ronnie, we are a family living in this house and we've tried to work it out so that we all respect each other's space and responsibility and privacy. Sandy is here so much that it's making us uncomfortable, because she's not really part of the family. We're not saying that we want you two to break up. We like Sandy and we believe you respect her and understand your responsibilities where sex is concerned. But we want our privacy back, and we'd like to know how you think we can solve this very important problem. We'll talk about it again in a few days, so please have some suggestions ready to talk about at that time."

This would be a side-by-side approach to the problem. Although the parents are firm, they do not turn the issue into a battlefield; the solutions that Ronnie comes up with will be the workable solutions precisely because they come from him and are not imposed upon him. The important thing in this or similar situations is to avoid turning the matter into an "either-or" stalemate.

What Ever Happened to Young Love?

A further worry for these parents, apart from the issue of their privacy, is the possibility of the two young people having sexual relations. Parents from time immemorial have worried about their children's sexual activities and the potential for untimely pregnancy, and today that fear is particularly well founded, with recent statistics showing a greater than ever rate of pregnancy occurring in unwed teenage girls.

Responsible parenting requires that parents talk candidly with their children about sex, but unfortunately many parents find it difficult to speak graphically about the physical aspects of love and desire—just as they find it difficult to be candid with themselves about their own sexual being. If they think or know that their children are having intercourse, they may assume that the kids have somehow learned—either from their friends or in sex education classes—about effective methods of contraception.

The proverbial embarrassment of parents in this matter is being complicated today by the highly emotional atmosphere surrounding the issue of abortion. Whether or not a woman has the right to abort an embryo or fetus and thus avoid bringing into the world a child that is not wanted has become a foremost and deeply divisive issue in family life, national politics, law, and medical practice.

Viewing the issue, I see truth in both positions, for and against abortion. And because it is not clear-cut, I can see no settlement of this issue in the near future; it will take time for a new ethic to evolve. Personally, I would hope that some solution other than abortion might be found in each and every case of unwanted pregnancy. I would prefer an ideal world in which every child might be conceived out of the need and desire of the parents to have that child, and where every pregnancy might come to fruition without surgical procedures being needed to rectify a "mistake." But the realities of our world are different.

I have seen young women who have had their babies outside of marriage and given them up for adoption at the cost of great emotional trauma that, even at the time I saw them some years later, was still not laid to rest.

Rarely have I seen a family where a daughter's "unwanted" child was integrated to the satisfaction of all concerned. There are the exceptions, of course. I have seen families in which a daughter's child has been in a sense adopted by the women in the family. It is almost as if the family needed another baby; the mother and a grandmother or aunt made it their business to raise and care for the child. In my view, such a child is a wanted child, one who fulfills a family need. But, in any case, for the "adoption" to be a satisfactory one, it is necessary for the family to be honest with the child about his or her parenthood. If the family tries to lie ("Daddy went away in the war" or some such fabrication), the lie will most certainly be found out and the unraveling of it will be a much bigger problem for the family than the problem of facing the truth openly in the beginning. But even where there is honesty, it usually takes a lot of work to help the growing child live with the fact that he has only one parent while all of his friends have two. The child will always wonder about the parent he never knew: Why was that parent excluded? Was he such a monster that knowing him would be worse than keeping him as a shadowy figure?

Often I talk with parents who say that their only child was conceived before they married—in some cases, even before they thought of marrying—and that the pregnancy influenced their decision to marry. I find in these marriages, almost without exception, substantial problems and a lack of resolution; it is as if the partners saw the marriage as something that was taken out of their hands. I can only wonder what these people would have been like if, by choosing an abortion, they had allowed themselves the necessary time to think about their relationship.

What is not acceptable, I feel, is the idea that abortion can be treated lightly, or that it is a problem for the woman alone. The simplicity of the procedure, in medical terms, does not equate with its psychological aspects, which are complex and difficult. The woman or girl who chooses to have an abortion will be helped immensely if her family supports her, understands her needs, and does not make her feel guilty about taking this step. The alternative to making it a family affair is to leave the woman to undergo the abortion more or less alone, which she will do out of the wish to spare her family pain. The sadness of the matter is then compounded by fear, guilt, and a sense of isolation. If abortion must be the choice, I would hope that in every case it might be done under the most helpful and supportive circumstances.

Will It Lead to Marriage?

All too soon the period of young love is over and parents find themselves viewing their children's lovers as potential marriage partners. Almost always they find ways to indicate their preferences, whether by conscious or unconscious moves.

Whatever their opinions may be, it is good policy for parents to stay out of the romantic entanglements of their adult children. It's even better policy for the children to keep their parents from being too well informed. A love affair should be a private affair. If it is shared prematurely with the family, and if the family approves, the system may try to incorporate it too soon; in other words, the two lovers may find themselves being encouraged to commit themselves before they are really ready to take that important step. This doesn't mean that a relationship shouldn't be shared with the family. It can be shared in appropriate ways and eventually the connection with family will need to be made, but only when the time is right.

It sometimes happens that parents see their child involved romantically with someone they strongly dislike or view as unsuitable. They fear the relationship will lead to unhappiness but they feel powerless to do anything about it. Even without intending it, however, parents are sometimes instrumental in ending a relationship. Their child casts them in this role by bringing home a lover so that the family will do what the child himself is unwilling or unable to do—that is, break up the relationship.

Susan Newman did this. She brought home a man she was thinking of marrying. He made the mistake of approaching her father on the subject of the material goods she would bring to the marriage and was practically thrown out of the house. As Susan's father put it, "I have no intention of making a financial deal with anyone for my daughter."

Can we suppose that Susan brought the young man home because she really thought her father would like him? Or that she did it to be spiteful? Neither explanation holds up. But in the systemic view, Susan's action makes sense. Her father's anger got her out of a situation about which she herself had deep, if unadmitted, reservations.

When a young person is too open about his or her romances, another problem often arises. Gail, who has been out of college about three years, is a good example. Gail brought home a succession of lovers to meet her parents, leaving her mother and father very confused about her intentions. Worse than that, they came to see her as promiscuous (in their day a young person did not go through a succession of lovers in order to find the right one). And once they began to think of their daughter as promiscuous, they applied the judgment to every relationship she formed and every man she brought home.

For many reasons, then, a degree of privacy is important if the love relationships of marriage-age children are to develop without familial pressures. And when the moment finally comes for lovers to be introduced to parents, the expectations on both sides should be realistic. Young people shouldn't expect their parents to fall in love with everyone *they* fall in love with; parents shouldn't expect every lover their child brings home to be the perfect partner they would wish for their child.

The Sexual Sleep-over and Other Modern *Mores*

Many parents today are confronted with questions of sexual *mores* that would have been unthinkable twenty years ago. They wonder about how to balance their parental responsibilities against the influence of a culture that seems to be saying "anything goes." Many see their kids taking lovers, living together, and sometimes having babies outside the civil and religious sanctions of marriage.

Parents can prepare themselves to handle these unsettling situations by agreeing on a stance that takes into account their moral values, their life-style, and their relationships with their individual children; and they have to be able to state that opinion clearly. Their responsibility is not to pronounce on right and wrong but to let it be known unmistakably what they think and feel.

The so-called sexual sleep-over is one of these questions.

When children are small they like having sleep-overs with their friends; usually these are kids of the same sex whom their parents know and approve of. When the children get older, the friends they bring home (still of the same sex) may intrude more on the family's home life,

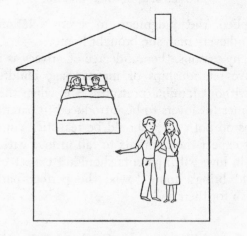

Today's parents have to deal with issues—like the sexual sleep-over—that would have been unthinkable when they themselves were young. Their responsibility is not to make pronouncements about what is right or wrong, but to let it be known unmistakably what they think and feel.

since they have their own norms and it takes a certain amount of accommodation on the family's part to make them feel at home.

Something quite different is happening with increasing frequency today. Young people are bringing home their lovers and expecting their parents to approve of them sharing the same bed. "We love each other and we sleep together at college," a twenty-year-old named Greg told his parents. "It's just hypocrisy to make Alice sleep in another room when she comes home with me."

Not too many parents are comfortable with the idea of sexual sleep-overs, especially when there are younger children in the household who haven't the level of maturity to understand why Greg and Alice are sleeping in the same bed.

What can parents say when their wishes run counter to

the wishes of their children in this matter? It's important to establish ground rules. One possible statement is this: "What you do outside the house is your own business, but we do not want your lover sleeping with you here at home. We understand that you are trying your wings but we don't want them tried at home. It's too difficult for us to deal with. It makes us uncomfortable."

A statement like that is firm, reasonable, and in keeping with the parents' belief system. Whatever their decision in the matter, it should be put to their child in that way.

Despite the sexual freedom that young people enjoy, they seem, if anything, more troubled than in previous times about their ability to fall in love and have intimate relationships. A great many are uncertain about their sexuality and about the institution of marriage. They say that it's easy to find a sexual partner but almost impossible to find somebody who is willing to make the commitment to a lasting relationship. (I assume that the young people we hear from are the ones who can't find their opposite number; those who *can* are probably never heard from.)

Certainly, the reasons for this confusion are many and complex. Many men feel threatened by the women's liberation movement and its search for equality in the home and workplace. Some respond by choosing a path that leaves them in control of their relationships rather than risk a commitment where they would have to face working out the issue of equality with a woman. And women, for their part, are becoming more reluctant to hand over control over their lives to a spouse.

Parents who view the confusion of their young with consternation and sadness are not entirely outside the situation. They may have it in their power to help their children form good relationships. A way to do this is to work constantly on their own relationship, to give a model of marriage in which there is change and adjustment throughout the stages of life, in which contentment outweighs dissatisfaction.

The Perils of Early Marriage

Most parents look with anticipation toward the time when the family will be enlarged by the addition of a daughter- or son-in-law and grandchildren.

Occasionally, in their eagerness to see a new unit bud off on the family tree, parents give their tacit approval to the marriage of two very young people. They look on the romance and see the beauty and the incandescence of it. They think of the families they know where the parents were high-school sweethearts and now have been married thirty or forty years and are celebrating anniversaries with their descendants. They feel confident that the same happy future lies in store for their own children.

Unfortunately, however, the divorce statistics are telling us a different story about early marriage. Counseling offices are filled with young people who wed at an early age and are now coming to the realization that something important is missing in their lives. They married before their emancipation from childhood had truly evolved, before they learned enough about life to prepare them for the responsibilities of family life. They know now that marriage is a far more complicated and restrictive state than they had expected, and they wonder how they can ever find the time and space to experience the missing pieces of their lives.

Early marriage is not an automatic entrée to adulthood and emancipation. If anything, it may make it harder for the young marrieds to evolve independence from their

LOVE, SEX, AND MARRIAGE

families of origin and to make secure connections to the
families they marry into.

Past Patterns and Future Compatibility

It seems to be a fact that when we marry, the person we
choose is exactly the person we need at that time in our
life. However odd the match may seem to outsiders, it
always makes sense in the context of the needs of the individuals involved. Each partner sees in the other something
that makes up for what they haven't acquired out of the
experience of living in their own families—an economic,
cultural, familial, or other kind of asset they feel will give
them completion. For instance, a couple may come together because one has an illness or a weakness and sees in
the spouse, or intended spouse, a caretaker who will provide support in the vicissitudes of the disease or weakness.
Or, a couple may come together from varying religious
backgrounds, hoping to find in each other a religiosity or a
faith they were unable to evolve out of their own family
backgrounds.

Although complementarity implies that the partners
differ in certain respects, differences are not always a sign
of complementarity. Often, people marry despite important and serious conflicts in their values and attitudes. If
they don't bridge these conflicts over time, building on
their complementarities and evolving their individuality,
the differences can become chasms that will eventually
cause them to break apart.

A certain pattern is notable among couples who come
for therapy because of trouble early in their marriage.
When the partners are questioned about their past family
lives, it usually comes out that in each case their parents

had difficult, involved, troubled marriages. Often I say to these couples, "Well, how can you know what a good marriage is? The only other marriages you know from the inside are your parents' marriages and they were unhappy. So, if you two want to have a good marriage, you are going to have to evolve one."

Even under the best of circumstances a happy marriage is not easy to evolve. Imagine a basic trainee from the American army and a basic trainee from the Russian army being suddenly brought together and sent out together on patrol. They have different weapons and equipment, different training techniques, different responses in different situations, different languages, even different meal rations. They have to learn to communicate before they can begin to cooperate.

This, in a way, is what happens when two people marry. They come from two different systems and their basic training for marriage is what they have learned by observing how their mothers, fathers, aunts, uncles, cousins, and grandparents all behaved and interrelated. When they marry, they start to evolve out of that knowledge a new homeostatic entity that reflects the patterns of their families' behaviors.

The Bairds are an interesting instance of family patterning. Kitty and Tom Baird have been married for twenty-eight years. Their three children are Joyce, twenty-six, Lynn, twenty-four, and Gary, sixteen.

Tom Baird is a sensitive man, an orthopedic surgeon. One evening, over drinks with an old family friend, he confessed a feeling of sadness about his daughters. "I'm sure that neither one has ever been in love," he said. "Oh, they have boyfriends, but I think there's a whole dimension of life that has somehow passed them by. Here they are, young and attractive, with good jobs, yet they've never been Juliet to anyone's Romeo, never had that exultation and pain. I sometimes wonder if they're going to live out their lives that way."

Dr. Baird has reason to worry. His marriage, although to all outward appearances a stable one, has problems that he and his wife have never really addressed.

Kitty and Tom are the products of diverse family influences. Her parents were strict and demanding. As a child, if Kitty behaved as anything less than a good and dutiful daughter, her mother would slap her. Then her mother would pass on the ill report to her father and he too would strike her. In this way Kitty's parents believed they were making her perfect. "No one will ever be good enough for you," her mother used to tell her.

The man Kitty chose to marry is caring, lovable, paternalistic, a man on whom others—including his own parents and siblings—have depended, a man incapable of punishing behavior toward his children. But he is also a man much taken up with work and other activities outside the family, and he expresses his giving nature largely in terms of material objects (clothes for his daughters, an expensive car for his wife). His strength and his aloofness have fostered his wife's dependency without providing the degree of companionship she needs. By now Kitty has arrived at a point in her life where she feels dissatisfied with herself, dissatisfied with her husband, and dissatisfied with her marriage.

The Baird daughters, meanwhile, are beset by ambivalence. They hear their mother's hidden message: "I thought I had found someone good enough, but I didn't and you won't either." Still, Joyce and Lynn see what they want to see in their father, someone on whom they can depend, and they measure their male friends against that image of strength. At the same time, they are influenced by a feminist ethic that tells them, "Be equal, don't be dependent."

The mixed feelings that struggle for dominance in Joyce and Lynn have prevented them from falling in love. Perhaps if we could read their hearts, we would find inscribed there the words their grandmother so often spoke to their mother: "No one will ever be good enough for you." If they *do* marry, it is almost certain that those words will echo again somewhere in their future family systems.

Thus the pattern is transferred. The conflict in these young women is a remarkable example of the way even absent grandparents are ghost presences in the emotional lives of later generations.

Connecting Back

Invariably, when I hear people complain of an emptiness in their marriage, I find that they feel an almost equal emptiness in their original familial relationships. It seems that we cannot expect to have a full, contented, complete life unless we have had a full, contented, complete past. The problem for most of us is that we have not had such happy pasts. What then? Is our situation hopeless?

In answer, I would say that most of us *do* have a way of helping ourselves in this situation. I think we can achieve some degree of comfort with our past by the process of connecting back. This means making contact with the members of one's original family and trying to resolve as far as possible any residual problems in family relationships. Written or spoken exchanges with a mother, father, and siblings are the first steps in this settlement process; if aunts and uncles and cousins can be included too, so much the better. (See chapter 10 for more on this process and how to go about it.)

For many of us connecting back is essential, for as long as our disconnections from important family members continue, and as long as those relationships are not resolved, we feel a sense of loss and dis-ease.

In the case of Nancy and Bill, a couple who came to therapy because of dissatisfaction with their marriage, connecting back was a clear and necessary move.

Nancy and Bill were in their mid-thirties, each of them married for a second time after unsuccessful, childless first marriages. They'd been married this time for about five years and were on the verge of divorce. They had a child, a little girl of about four.

Here again the rule proved out. Both Nancy and Bill came from families where there was little show of love or affection but much conflict and discontent. Both of Bill's parents and his younger sister were alive. He was out of touch with his parents and only occasionally in touch with his sister. Nancy's father was dead; her mother, who had remarried about six years before, rarely saw her daughter, and when the two women did meet, they were uncomfortable with each other. Nancy had no siblings; she was an only child.

I put this couple to work communicating with their relatives. With my help, Nancy started writing to her mother, who lived in Kansas City. The letters were newsy and included gentle probing questions that we hoped would cause her mother to write back with information about her life and about life in the family when Nancy was small.

With Bill, I asked him to have occasional lunches alone with his sister and to try to talk about family history, being careful to avoid the subjects that in the past had always led to arguments between them. I asked him also to find occasions when he could be alone and talk with each of his parents.

After following through on this program over a period of months, both Nancy and Bill felt much more comfortable in their family connections. What is more, they were better able to connect with each other. Indeed, the more they learned about their families and their pasts, the brighter became their chances of being able to change.

Marriage as a Rite of Passage

Family therapy reveals how some of the so-called independence moves that young people make really have nothing to do with independence. Often they are ill-fated attempts to break free of painful relationships. I am referring here particularly to elopement.

Consider, for example, a young couple who come from very troubled family backgrounds: the man from a home that is filled with conflict; the woman from parents who are totally dependent people—a mother and father so enmeshed with each other that it would be difficult to think of them as separate individuals. In seeking to do the right thing, these two young people see only one possibility —to run off and get married with none of the family being present at the wedding.

Unfortunately, what these two do by eloping is a complete misunderstanding of what they need to do to get free of the dis-ease they feel. By creating such a great distance between themselves and their families, they make it very difficult to evolve truly independent positions for themselves. Moreover, their relationship with each other can only suffer as a result of the disconnection from family.

To couples who are thinking of eloping, I would make the point that families need their tribal rites. You cannot truly progress out of your families of origin into a new family without going through the rites of passage. You cannot simply run away and get married and thereby *be* married. You may satisfy the legal requirements, but the systemic budding off will not have taken place. Without the wedding occasion, your families will have no way of recognizing and confirming that a marriage has really happened.

In a way, a wedding is like a barn-raising and the family guests are like the pillars that will hold the new structure up. People need familial pillars to help support the edifice of their life—not just pillars in the middle, but pillars all around. That's how we build a building and that's what keeps it up. When those pillars are weak, that building is likely to collapse from the shaking life gives it.

A Little Less Than Married

A woman at a small dinner party was describing her dilemma to the other guests at the table. The girl her son was living with was about to have a birthday and she couldn't decide whether or not she should give the girl a present. From the spate of responses she got it was clear she had touched a sensitive subject: the tenuous relationships between parents and their children's nonformalized partners.

Something relatively new and phenomenal in our present-day culture is the number of young people who are cohabiting without being married to each other. While there is much to be said for the experience of living together, it must also be recognized that the experience is loaded with confusion for everyone. It brings up questions of commitment, sharing, legal status, as well as the question that concerns us here: how to be a quasi in-law.

Recently I attended the wedding of the daughter of a

woman I have known since childhood. The bride and groom had been living together for three years before this event, and in all that time my friend, Marion, had held herself aloof from the relationship, even refusing to visit the couple in their apartment—and this despite the fact that in all respects the young man was a very desirable match for her daughter.

Knowing Marion as I do, I could understand her attitude. Her upbringing was such that she simply could not accept the fact of these young people living together without the customary legal and religious sanctions. I knew, too, that her estrangement from her daughter, though not complete, had been very hard on her emotionally. During the reception (an especially happy one because the young people seemed so perfectly matched), Marion said to me, "Now I can sleep."

Some might judge this mother to have been stiff-necked and censorious in her disapproval of the living-together. I am not of this opinion. I think that her honesty probably had much to do with the joyous outcome.

Throughout it all, Marion remained herself. She attempted nothing that was beyond her capabilities. She didn't visit the couple because she *couldn't* visit them. She remained the person her daughter knew her to be. Had she gone to the apartment she might have blighted the place and the relationship with her unspoken (or outspoken) resentment. On the contrary, the message implicit in her course of conduct was that she would prefer her daughter to be married to this man—a very different message from "I don't like him."

When parents have to choose between their child's beliefs and their own beliefs, they should do only what they feel comfortable doing. They may shake their heads at their child's life-style or choice of a lover, but the truth about mating is that we choose our lovers according to our needs. We live with the person we need at a certain moment in our lives, marry whom we need at a certain moment, divorce at the moment we need someone or something else. These needs are not mere expressions of selfishness; they have to do with being the person we are. To contradict our needs in favor of the needs of others is not generosity; it merely leads to confusion in relationships.

When parents feel torn, they should keep their own needs, and not their children's needs, in the forefront because, in truth, they don't know what the needs of their children really are. As long as they remain the same people their children know, the children will be able to handle situations of conflict. It's when parents seem to be changing their belief system that their children become confused. What's more, it is a waste of effort for parents to try to conform themselves to their child's way of thinking. Any time they try to do something differently from the way they have always done it, they are going to do it wrong— for sure. (Witness the embarrassment of children when they see their middle-aged parents trying to act "groovy.")

So then, what about the quandary of the woman who wondered whether or not she should give her son's lover a birthday present?

Clearly she was uncomfortable with the idea of making this gesture. Yet she persisted, very likely because she felt unconsciously that if she treated the girl as a daughter-in-law, eventually she would *have* her as a daughter-in-law and the anxieties she felt over the living-together would be relieved. (Obviously she liked the girl or she wouldn't have thought of giving her a present.)

In the end, the woman asked her son what to do. He said simply, "Don't give her a present." She followed his advice, and by settling the matter this way, she found some of the comfort she was looking for.

In some cases, living together without marrying is as far as two people really want to go in their commitment to each other. Yet they may go ahead and get married because one or the other or both believe that the legalization will somehow change things for the better. The same thinking often leads childless couples to have a baby ("It will stabilize the marriage") and other couples to have a second or third child ("It will complete the family"). So the partners take the step and afterward find that their relationship has not really changed.

One couple who came to me for therapy had lived together for a year, during which, they said, they did a lot of fighting. Although there were profound differences between them—of values, religious beliefs, and social abilities—these two chose one seemingly insignificant issue to fight over: she liked to eat in French restaurants and he hated French restaurants.

They did get married, but within a month's time they were ready to file for a divorce.

It would be easy to say that this was a stupid marriage and that it should never have taken place. But my premise is that people do what they do for their own and for other people's well-being, so we have to try to see how this particular marriage was indeed well-intentioned. I came to the conclusion that for these two people marriage was actually a way of ending their unhappy relationship. They needed to take it to the full extent, to legalize it and to legally divorce.

If two people have trouble with each other after they

marry, we can be sure they had trouble before they married. Marriage itself neither makes nor breaks a relationship.

The Childless Option

Steve and Deborah were a young married couple who came to therapy because they were quarreling a lot and had just separated. He owned a restaurant and she worked full time in the administration office of a hospital. Early in their relationship she would meet him at his restaurant after work and they'd have dinner and perhaps go to a movie and then go home together. But they had stopped having these evenings out. And they'd more or less given up their custom of going off and spending Sundays together in some pleasant place. Also, they were at odds over how to share their money: what was his was his, what was hers was hers. They didn't even have a home in the true sense. She had moved into his apartment and had gone on thinking of it as *his* apartment. For a long time she'd find things there that belonged to his former girl friend, and this brought home to her how little she and Steve had of a real marriage.

The problem for Steve and Deborah was not that they needed to spend more time together or share more experiences. The problem as I saw it was, Are they a family? Do they want to be a family? If they are a family, do they want children? And if so, when are they going to have children? These two had carried the confusions of the courtship stage over into the married state: they were reluctant to commit themselves to each other and to their future. Like many of their generation, they wished to remain free "for a few years," and the choice had somehow led to a narrowing-down of their lives. They had their two-ness to occupy them and not very much more.

Thinking of Steve and Deborah raises the question of why some couples decide not to become a family, not to have children. Is it a thoughtful decision they make about their lives? Do they think children are difficult to bring up? Do they fear the responsibilities of parenting? (To be sure, the responsibilities of raising a family *are* great. Although it is said that one's first responsibility is to one's self, when we marry and have children, this has to be interpreted differently. Once we bring a child into the world, for the formative years of that child's life until he or she leaves home, that child is our first responsibility.)

It's my belief that in many cases the decision to remain childless has little to do with such considerations. Rather, I think it expresses the way the two partners view the world. Unconsciously they reject any role in the process of continuing their family, so they become part of the process of family extinction.

Yes, families can and do become extinct. For reasons that are not easily explained, the birth rate in such a family lowers to the point where it no longer renews itself as members marry. The family peters out. Understood systemically, we could say that extinction becomes a way of life in that family.

To me there is a great sadness about the choice of remaining childless. It is almost as if these couples are saying, "We're going to be a party to ending the world." My wish for all who marry is that they might believe in life strongly enough to want to see it carried forward into the future.

6

DIVORCE AND THE
SINGLE-SPOUSE FAMILY

Today we are seeing many marriages of fifteen, twenty, and twenty-five years' duration breaking up or struggling to survive. Many of these long-standing marriages are on the rocks because the partners haven't been able to grow and change in their relationship. They have allowed an atmosphere of boredom and sameness to build up and now they find that the satisfactions of marriage—in the way of mutual support, sexual fulfillment, lack of loneliness—are no longer enough to outweigh the dissatisfaction in their lives. In an earlier time many of these husbands and wives might have chosen to go on with their marriages for the "sake of the children," but in today's moral climate they feel free to divorce, and they are doing so in great numbers.

With this rise in the failure rate among marriages of long standing, it is obvious that many of the children involved are in their transitional years or older—the age group we are particularly concerned with in this book. However, because divorce is a systemic breakdown that causes pain to everyone in the family, it would be impractical to try to separate out the problems of the adult children in parental divorce or separation. To return to the image of the family as an edifice, we might say that in divorce it is the parental pillars that fail, causing the entire building to sag or collapse. Thus, any therapeutic approach to the problems of divorce and separation should be one that takes all family members into account, one that tries to use the pillars and connectors of the broken family to construct a new and workable family system, so that the sense of family, which we need so much in our lives, will be able to survive the trauma of divorce.

Can a Family Survive Divorce?

How, you might wonder, can a family survive such severe trauma? Almost everything about divorce works against the idea and the reality of family. A family means a unit of mother, father, and offspring living in a household and cooperating to meet their various needs. Divorce, on the other hand, means the scattering of family members into two households; instead of cooperating, they often engage in conflict over money, property, custody of children, and visitation rights; instead of governing their own life as a family, they bring in the law to arbitrate their quarrels.

The children of divorce have their security profoundly undermined. They live with the fear of loss, then with the actuality of it when the parents finally part. They have to divide their loyalties between their mother in one place and their father in another place. They lose the sense of belonging to a unit (their family), which they need in order to grow and mature. If they see that one parent has a lover while the other is left alone and depressed, the seeming unfairness of that situation may make them angry and judgmental. And they get no adequate answer to their persistent question, "Why?" (A family therapist I know recently went through divorce—yes, it even happens to

Divorce is a systemic breakdown that causes pain to everyone in the family. Little that is positive can come from it unless the family members are able to reconnect with each other in a newly structured family system—unlike the figures above, who remain disconnected and unresolved in their relationships.

family therapists—and when he told his children about the impending separation he was abashed to hear his son say accusingly, "Listen, you're a family therapist, so why didn't you and Mom try family therapy before you decided to split?")

The parents, too, suffer from divorce in ways they may not have anticipated. Although the parting satisfies some of their needs, the satisfaction cannot initially balance the powerful feeling of loss. The noncustodial parent feels an emptiness in the place once occupied so fully by children. The divorced partners feel the loss of the families they had joined (indeed, some patients in therapy feel the estrangement from their in-laws as if it were an amputation, with all the trauma that goes with the loss of a bodily limb). They feel the loss of friendships they shared with other couples and individuals.

Simply bringing family members together does not dis-

pel the sense of systemic dis-ease after divorce. Family
gatherings are likely to be occasions of discomfort rather
than joy. For example, the wedding of a son or daughter
can become a family battleground instead of a family reunion, with reproaches flying back and forth between the
divided families. Children, not realizing the reasons for
their actions, often do things in order to avoid family gatherings. We earlier gave the example of the young person
about to graduate college at the time of his parents' divorce who dropped out of school in order to avoid the confrontation that might otherwise occur at his graduation.

Perhaps the most tragic aspect of divorce is that families
often go through all this—the loss, anger, sadness, and
financial hurt of divorce—without ever finding the comfort
or happiness they hoped to attain by it. They seem to get
very little that is positive out of the experience.

Finishing the Marriage and Re-forming the Family

A divorce need not miscarry in this way. I believe a divorce can have the hoped-for positive results *provided* the
parties to it refuse to accept the dissolution of the family
as a necessary part of the divorce process, and instead
regroup themselves after divorce in a form that incorpo-
rates all of the parts of the old family structure. (Actually,
the word *divorce* is not correct to describe what happens in
the breakup of a long-term marriage. Separate residences
may be established, new partners may be brought in, but
divorce in the absolute sense does not occur. Personal ties
remain, and one way or another they continue to be felt by
the people involved.)

I use the word re-formation to describe the process of
restructuring that needs to take place after divorce. Re-formation means that the divorced husband and wife cooper-

ate to resolve their broken relationship in a way that keeps the unit of mother-father-offspring viable although functioning along new and different lines. If a divorce occurs and the restructuring does not, then the divorce will be incomplete and the positive results will never be gained.

To describe re-formation it might be useful to return to the image of the family as an edifice. Imagine an office building that seems well planned on the drawing board but when finally erected proves to be flawed in some way that affects its functioning—in its design, communication system, location, or some other aspect. Because of this and other forces at work, the building in time becomes less and less desirable and the tenants leave one by one until the place becomes a bare and empty structure whose systems are inoperative. For this building to survive, the owners have to bring in new tenants, but first they have to renovate the structure to meet the particular requirements of the new tenants. They strip the building down to its framework, until only the columns and connecting beams remain. Then the builders put in new inner walls, add an extra story, and attach a new outer skin to the framework of the structure. When the new tenants move in they furnish their space to suit their own needs and tastes. The original skeleton of the building is still there, its connections still in force and still giving support. Instead of being demolished, the building is given a new life.

In somewhat the same way, when a family re-forms after divorce, it may be unrecognizable from its original appearance but it still functions to provide a sense of security and support to the family members. Instead of wastefully destroying what was good in their relationships they keep their connections with each other while changing the design of their lives and perhaps adding new members to the system.

That re-formation can help in the aftermath of divorce was dramatically demonstrated in the case of a family I will call the Iversons. After Jane and Ken Iverson were divorced, their sixteen-year-old son, Jeremy, began to show serious disturbances. He had trouble keeping friends, was insolent to his teachers, and was picked up for vandalizing a neighbor's property. When his parents began to find new partners he couldn't get along with them; on one or two occasions he even threatened to hit his father's new wife.

In family therapy, Jane and Ken were helped in the work of finishing their broken marriage. They came to accept that the marriage was really over and that it was time to admit and allow each other's faults. They realized that if they continued to fight over the issues outstanding between them, particularly about the parenting of Jeremy, they would never really be divorced and their son would never be free to grow and evolve in a new situation.

As the divorced parents learned to cooperate on their residual problems and to talk to each other without tension and bitterness, Jeremy's acting-out behavior decreased markedly. His hostility toward his parents' new partners almost disappeared and he learned to relate to them as adult friends and as parental figures. Although Jane and Ken were having trouble in their new relationships, the trouble they had dealing with each other became less and less of a factor in the enlarged family system. They achieved enough elasticity in the new system so that Jeremy could move easily between the two families—spending comfortable time with his father (who had conceded custody), visiting his paternal grandparents, and eventually getting on friendly terms with his stepmother.

Up to this point I have been speaking to parents, mothers and fathers who are separating or divorcing and who are concerned about the effects of the experience on their maturing children. But there is another generation to consider too: the parents of the divorcing partners.

People whose marriages are breaking up often try to keep their parents in ignorance of the fact. They are discreet about their quarrels and differences, and when the decision to divorce is finally made they may put off telling their parents about it as long as they can.

There is no way I know of to sugar-coat this revelation, and there is no point in holding it back. As soon as the divorcing partners are sure in their minds, they should tell their parents—but not without looking for the right words and the right circumstances in which to do it.

Parents tend to react in extreme ways to the news of an impending divorce. They may be vehemently opposed to or vehemently in favor of the divorce. They may seem surprised or else say that they were always sure it would work out this way. They may be saddened or relieved. If they seem to react inappropriately, it is only their way of trying to deal with the dislocations, separations, and changes in relationships that will follow in the wake of the divorce. The family that is breaking up may have come to form a significant part of their lives, and like the children of the marriage, the parents too may feel divided loyalties and the uncomfortable urge to place blame in the situation. When divorce results in the breaking off of relationships that have formed in the course of the marriage, everyone feels a great sense of loss. Severances of this sort should be avoided, if possible, by the process of family re-formation.

The Step-Family System

Re-formation is an even more complex process when the divorced parents remarry, as is happening with great frequency these days. The geometrics of a nuclear family are complicated enough, but when we add in the members of an entirely new system (new stepsiblings, aunts, uncles, grandparents), not to mention a new parent, the complexity becomes vastly greater. And there are even more variables to be considered: the stage in family life when divorce and remarriage occurred, the geographical distance between the divorced partners, the frequency and quality of visits between members of the two families, and so forth.

When two family systems are suddenly superimposed upon one another, as in the step-family, relationships feel disjointed. A phone call from an ex-spouse may cause jealousy in the new partner; children may resent their new parents and feel ill at ease with their new siblings; it may be difficult for a parent to discipline a stepchild and to keep from showing partiality to his or her own child; in-laws may interfere in matters that shouldn't (you think) concern them.

What I said earlier about re-forming the family unit after divorce applies equally to re-formation of the step-family. The families that one or both partners belonged to before they remarried have to be able to find a place in the new, expanding system. ("Family" here includes parents and other in-laws as well as children and ex-spouses.)

It is especially important for new parental figures to understand their stepchildren's loyalty to their biological parents and to honor those connections. What a child in a step-family needs most of all is to be able to accept the new family without letting his contacts with the original family members interfere. He may think of the pre-divorce unit as his real family, but he now needs to be able to live in both families—the old and the new.

An older child in a newly forming step-family may feel

that his parent, by remarrying, is saying in effect, "Now I want to take care of me, now I can be free," and he may respond to that by seeming to move more quickly than he otherwise would toward separation. He could be making a false start in life, however, if there are issues and problems in the family that remain unresolved. I would emphasize, therefore, the need to make offspring who are in their later teens or older feel that they truly belong to the step-family.

As stepparents, our responsibility to our older children is not diminished. We have to help them evolve their maturity and feel that they have connections to a living, enduring family. Divorce and remarriage are difficult passages for the family to weather, but with good will and lots of work on everyone's part they can lead on to calmer seas.

Decision-Making in Single-Spouse Families

What of those parents who are raising families alone as a result of death, divorce, or separation in the marriage? They have all the usual problems, plus some others that have to do particularly with their status as single spouses.

One of these problem areas is decision-making. I am thinking here of a recently divorced mother whose daughter, Dorothy, on turning sixteen began asking permission to stay out much later than the twelve-thirty curfew her mother and father had set the year before, while they were still married.

Dorothy's mother, Eve, who had shown considerable strength and resilience since the day her husband announced he wanted a divorce, promised Dorothy that she would think about it.

Although she felt capable of handling this matter alone, Eve telephoned her ex-husband and asked him for his opinion on the matter. On the following weekend, he stopped by the house, and the three of them sat down over coffee in the kitchen and talked—about many things but especially about resetting Dorothy's curfew time. Dorothy described her embarrassment and the inconvenience she felt she was causing her friends by having to start home by midnight. But when she saw her parents united in their concern for her, she was less inclined to push her request too far. In the end it was she who settled the matter, agreeing to come home by 1 A.M. on regular weekend dates, with extra time to be allowed for special parties.

Unfortunately, in many households where a single spouse is trying to do the work of two, this kind of decision-making does not go on. The mother—who is usually the spouse nominated to live with the children—may or may not have been the limit-setter when the family was intact, but now she has to be homemaker as well as sole source of discipline in such important matters as the children's schooling, dating, hours, traveling, and so forth. Some single spouses feel it to be an overwhelming responsibility.

It is a mistake, I believe, for the custodial parent to assume the entire burden of making important decisions. As far as possible, those decisions should be a source of concern and responsibility for both parents; as with Dorothy's family, everyone concerned should have a voice in the negotiating process. (If the absent spouse can't be present at the discussion, his or her views can be made clear by letter or phone.) If the parents don't agree, then they have to be clear with each other and with their children about their disagreement and present it logically to their grown children when it comes up for discussion with them. With a young child, the parents needn't necessarily discuss every limitation or decision, but they do need to be clear with each other about how much latitude their child will be given.

Suppose the absent spouse is someone who seems chronically inclined to poor judgment and irresponsibility? Should he or she have a voice in decisions?

Yes. Even in the case of a parent like this, it is still necessary for his or her wishes to be considered. The children are going to have to deal with that person in their future lives and there is nothing to be gained by shielding them from the truth about a parent's weaknesses.

Guilt Feelings of the Single Spouse

Guilt feelings are another problem the single parent must try to overcome. Unfortunately, they get little help in this from society at large. For example, while this book was in preparation, newspapers carried mention of a study released by an association of educators that upheld the theory that children from broken homes suffer disadvantages; their school performance was judged to be below normal as compared to that of children from intact families.*

I must comment on this, because I cannot imagine what good these educators hoped to bring about by publishing their conclusions. In confirming a long-held belief, the report could not be said to have broken new ground. Nor did it do anything appreciable to ease the pain and confusion of the children who were its subjects. Instead, parents who read or hear of these statements are likely to blame themselves for their children's problems in school. That guilt, I believe, is the most notable result of a report like this and of the publicity given to it.

Acting out in school is certainly one of the ways in

---

* Report released in 1980 by the National Association of Elementary School Principals.

which kids react to the trauma of divorce, and parents and teachers should respond to that cry for help as they would in any case—whether divorce was part of the problem or not. Parents can also remind themselves, in this situation, that their kids are not doomed to fail in life because of the divorce. We can all look back to people we knew in school who came from "stable families," who were never absent, who never made trouble, and who, in fact, never seemed to do much of anything—either as school children or as mature adults. Stable family relationships are much to be desired, but by themselves they are no guarantee of future success and happiness.

When Children Protect Their Parents

When a mother is left to parent her family alone, it often happens that the children become overprotective of her. A family I will call the Kennedys are a good example of this.

Lisa Kennedy has five children. The oldest, at twenty-one, is Al, Jr., who has recently gotten an entry-level job in communications that necessitates a daily commute to the city by train. Between him and his youngest sibling, twelve-year-old Tom, are Kelly, nineteen, Meg, seventeen, and Laurie, fourteen, all students at local schools. The Kennedys have just moved to a smaller house; it's nice, but it is nonetheless a much smaller house than the one they had before Al, Sr., died suddenly last year at age forty-six of heart disease.

In the months since his death, the family has struggled to evolve its collective future and the future of each of the family members. Lisa has found a full-time job in a law office, and the children are performing well in school. The major focus of attention is young Al, who cannot decide whether or not to move to the city to live. He is making thirteen thousand dollars a year, which he says is not enough to enable him to live in the city, even with a sharing arrangement. He commutes, being driven to and from the station by his mother. The casual observer might suppose him to be another husband being met at the train by his wife. At home Al has moods that often erupt into verbal battles with his mother. He says he wants to leave and she encourages him to leave, yet he doesn't go. The atmosphere in the house is so tense that Lisa fervently wishes he would go.

The death of Al Kennedy has had tremendous impact on his family—psychologically, economically, and socially. What has particular relevance to our subject here, however, is the relationship between Lisa and her oldest son. It has parallels in many families where children, out of an overwhelmingly strong motivation, rush in to fill what they perceive to be the needs of a now-incomplete parent. When this happens, the parent-child relationship takes on a different dynamic. As the child becomes more helpful, the mother may relate to her child as she did to her spouse. If the mother gives up any of her competence and her ability to cope, this will only increase the child's helping efforts. Children in this position may eventually feel imprisoned by their parent's needs. Not only will they stick around the nest; they will get more and more glued into it.

Children do not see that the need for which they are sacrificing themselves is more a perception than a reality. "Mother needs help," they believe, and so, being the helpful animals they are, they rush to her aid. In reality, what the mother needs is to pass through her pain and loneliness and emerge from the other side of her trial so that she will be able to evolve her future self. In trying to protect her from this experience, the children are actually doing their mother a disservice. Their helping turns into hindering.

The single spouse should be on guard to prevent this process from occurring. In Lisa's case, she needs to become aware of what is happening and to work out with her family a timetable for the years ahead so that the children, beginning with Al, will be able to plan on when they are going to move out and how they all will try to prepare themselves for an independent life.

(Although I have described a mother in the above instance, there are plenty of single men heading families these days, and what I've said applies equally to them.)

Sex and the Single Spouse

The single spouse should be free to seek a new partner and to lead a sexual life, yet this is often difficult because of the reactions of the children.

Sometimes younger children respond by trying to protect their castle from invasion; they may refuse to relate to an outsider or make it clear that they wish that person would go away. Or their efforts may go in the opposite direction; they may try desperately to pull the outsider in because they feel their mother or their father needs that person.

Efforts by children in either direction can present monumental problems for an outsider. Many a potential partner has been scared off because of the pressures the system sets up in this situation.

Part of the problem for offspring at this time is that they now see their parents as sexual beings, whereas before they probably thought of their parents as being on their last legs, sexually and otherwise. This is particularly so in families where sex was seldom if ever mentioned during the time the family was intact.

Older children certainly are aware of their own sexuality, but it can come as a shock to them to discover that their parents too have sexual impulses and needs. Children may make poignant attempts to set limits on their parents' sexuality. (I am reminded here of a ten-year-old girl who objected to her divorced father bringing home his girl friend to sleep over. The father wanted to arrive at some understanding with his daughter so that she wouldn't be upset, and he said to her, "Under what rules would it be okay if Mabel came and slept over?" She thought for a while and said, "Well, if your door's not locked and you and Mabel don't take your clothes off. Or if Mabel sleeps on the couch in the living room, then it's okay with me.")

The difficulty for parents is not merely in how they can have a sexual life or experiment with relationships. They may worry that if their adolescent children see them being sexual with someone the children will take it to mean that they too can do the same thing.

Single parents feel a very heavy responsibility to do "the right thing" in bringing up their children. They may try to overmanage life and to overlook the simpler solutions to problems. In the matter of their own sexual life, it is probably best in most cases for parents to be honest in saying just what the situation is. When a parent is having a series of romances and the child is thinking, "What's going on?" the parent should be able to say in effect, "This is what I need, this is me, this is what I am going to do. I am still your parent and you are still my child, so please try to understand."

I think most children are able to understand romance, especially when they see it as a loving relationship con-

ducted openly and without guilt. They probably will be
disturbed, however, if they see a parent involved with frequent successive lovers or concurrently with two or three
lovers. If a parent feels the need to have two or more relationships going on at the same time, these might best be
conducted in private to spare children from having to deal
with something they would have trouble understanding.

A single parent who feels frank and morally at ease
about having a love affair may be confronted with a dilemma when his or her grown child asks to bring home a
lover to stay over. Suddenly, what's right for Mom or Dad
is not right for Johnny or Doris. (I'm speaking of those
people who are confused by today's changing values. Some,
of course, are not confused; they adhere to strict moral and
ethical rules and wouldn't dream of letting their children
bring home someone of the opposite sex to sleep over unless the young people were married or, at the very least, engaged.)

For a parent in this situation, the answer will probably
not be found in concepts of right and wrong, but rather in
evolving a position the parent is least uncomfortable with.
Children can adjust to almost anything if they have a clear
understanding of what is happening and what is required
of them. You may say no, or you may say yes. The important thing is to choose a way you are comfortable with and
to explain that any other way would cause you to feel an
intolerable level of dis-ease and discomfort.

7

THE SOCIAL MATRIX:
PATTERNS OF EQUALITY

The women's movement is bringing about a different state of mind in the family. At the heart of the matter are the changing self-images of family members. People are asking themselves, What is the proper role of a mother in today's world? Of a father? The present generations are having to work out the answers to these questions largely without guidance from the past. Men are taking on more of the work of nurturing, with little to guide them in the patterns they learned from their own fathers, who were bread-winners first and nurturers second—if they nurtured at all. Women are participating more in the world outside the home; they are no longer willing to carry the load of house-hold responsibility by themselves. As their revolution progresses we will see its influence on all segments of society, but particularly on the family.

The movement of a mother and a father toward equality, if completed in a way that is satisfactory to them, can head off many familial problems. Just as important, it gives an example to children of the possibilities of a balanced relationship. In an atmosphere of equality, children may sooner grasp that their dependency on their parents is a

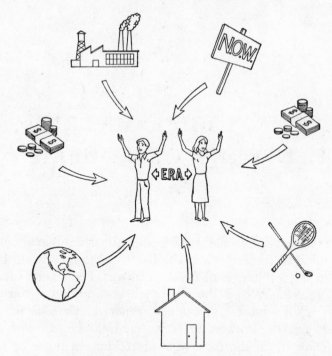

The movement toward sexual equality has meant a redefinition of family responsibilities. Some men feel that too much is being taken away from them; some women feel that too much is being asked of them. Nevertheless, the movement of a mother and father toward equality—if completed in a way that is satisfactory to them—can head off many familial problems.

temporary condition, that they can't operate as babies forever, but that they, too, need to evolve and mature and become adults in the family.

You may ask, what kind of equality can there be in a traditionally hierarchical, undemocratic structure like the family? Who has the right to do what, to be what? This issue of rights is probably the most difficult of all for families to work out.

Establishing Patterns of Equality

The traditional approach to child-rearing has not favored equality. The child entered the family as the mother's responsibility, and the effect of that was to put the couple in a kind of artificial balance with each other: the mother and the child on one side, the husband (and his work) on the other side.

Some couples today are looking at married life in a radically different way. By the time their baby is born, they have talked over their needs and decided how they might cooperate to share as equally as possible in raising the baby. Usually in these relationships the woman has given a clear message from the beginning: "I'm working and you're working, and even if the dollars coming in are not the same, we will have equal access to the family income. There are a certain number of household jobs that need doing, and we divide them up fairly."

Unfortunately, however, this is not a very widespread phenomenon. What we are seeing instead are couples who began life together in the traditional way and are trying now to dismantle the foundation of inequality on which they have built their marriages. Can it be done? I think so. What it means, if we look at it structurally, is that the system changes its distances: the mother moves her child (or children) somewhat away from her and closer to her husband. When the child is at an equal distance from both parents, and able to move as easily toward father as toward mother, the possibility exists for dividing the work of parenting more equally.

In making her move toward equality, the woman (assuming it is the woman who has been "less equal") has to be loud and clear in stating what she wants to do. Let's say her child is beginning school full time and she wants to take a job or return to school, and she sees that in order to do so she has to establish equal parenting with her husband: she must make the strong move of saying, "I will carry no more than fifty percent of the tasks of caring for our child [or children]." Then she will have to stand up to her husband's initial response ("Impossible, you know I can't be home before seven") by pointing out helpfully where there is time available in the mornings and evenings and on the weekends and insisting that he devote some of it to the child-rearing activities. She shouldn't expect him to be immediately willing to cooperate, however. Her husband will try to keep her as the major provider of services and so will her child. She will need to say to both of them, "I'm going to be living my life differently from now on." Because the wife originally helped put herself in a less powerful position, now it is up to her to choose and insist on the difference.

If we were to listen to husbands and wives as they speak about these moves, we might hear the inequality in operation:

Husband to wife: "Oh, I'd be happy to pay your tuition."

Husband to friends: "I want her to get out and work," or "I think it's marvelous, she's going back to school, I'm so glad she's doing that."

The husband here is "giving" something to his wife; it is not the language of equality.

When equality occurs it is through exchanges in which the person "below" takes a new position, while the person "above," the person spoken to, hears and responds appropriately. Thus, we would hear the wife saying, "I'm going to go back to school" and her husband telling friends, "Yes, my wife has decided to go back to school," or "My wife is starting her new job so I'm arranging my business differently." Here the relationship is beginning to be more nearly equal.

The need to try to evolve this change is real and pressing. In families where the mother sees that her worth lies only in nurturing children, she will tend to go on nurturing and taking responsibility even at the time when her adolescent child should be taking responsibility for practically all of his or her own actions. This is the pattern in many dependent families where the members are tied to each other. When separation occurs in these families, it is likely to be a mirage, not a true emancipation of the young person.

The so-called empty-nest syndrome has motivated many women to strive for equality by taking up work or activities outside the home. Had they done this ten or twenty years earlier, it might have been less difficult. But now the struggle can be a very stressful one; it has brought many marriages of twenty or twenty-five years to the brink of dissolution. An important part of the problem is the parents' fear of being alone, of having to face each other without an adolescent in the home whose energetic life force constantly needs to be dealt with. If there have been issues of parity between the husband and wife, these now come to the fore. And if the inequality has been going on too long, it may be too late in the marriage to change it. Unfortunately, the marriage pattern that grown children learn from such parents is one of dependency and dissatisfaction.

Patterns tend, as we have said, to reproduce themselves from generation to generation, and thus we cannot realistically expect family equality to come about overnight. Even where partners are strongly in agreement that they will strive for an equal division of responsibility and income, stereotypical notions tend to fog up their view.

I am reminded of a couple who came to therapy in hopes of saving their marriage. The wife, who had been married once before (her mother had been married *four* times), kept saying, "I want to be able to be dependent on my husband."

Now, I think there was a time in our society when marriages like this worked—at least to outside appearances. The woman was dependent on the man and the man wanted her to be dependent and he had liberties in return for carrying the financial responsibilities. The woman accepted this arrangement, even though she may have been consumed by resentment.

Today, a woman who struggles for any sense of her own identity has difficulty accepting a dependent position. That young woman, and others whose goal in marriage is "to be dependent," may never find the contentment they dream of.

Many young women today are making remarkable gains, yet some are still looking to marriage as a panacea, something that will save them from the work of evolving themselves. Like their mothers, many of whom aimed to be engaged—if not married—by the time they graduated from college, these young women have a basic misunderstanding of the institution of marriage. It is fine to marry because you don't want to live alone—most of us are not designed for living alone—but to marry because you think it will solve your problems is a mistake.

It may take many generations for us to grow out of the stereotypes that our families have handed down to us. This is as true for men as for women, and it partly explains why men so greatly outnumber women in administrative jobs. From time immemorial women have been the homemakers and men have been the hunters. Perhaps what men are really doing in their business suits is going out to kill the meat so they can bring it home and sit in front of the fire and eat themselves full. (The great entrepreneurs are the ones who know how to kill the big game.) Up until now women have not characterized themselves by this kind of aggressive ability. It is still the rare woman who claims a place in the boardroom.

How we unconsciously perpetuate this division was brought home to me one day as I listened to a young couple arguing about the housework.

She: "It's unequal, we're not doing the same amount of work in the house."

He: "We are so—you're crazy!"

The work was certainly not being shared equally by these two, and not just because the husband wasn't willing to cooperate. His wife was having trouble handing over her responsibilities (the domestic chores) to him. She was giving him the unconscious message that he couldn't do things as well as she could, and he was *not* doing them as well, and she was getting angry and doing them herself.

She: "The pots aren't as clean as when I clean them."

He: "They're clean enough!"

She: "No, I have to do them again."

Equality will happen when women take power for themselves. For an equality move to work, the person in the "lower" position must force the issue; equality cannot be bestowed. Until now women have not been allowed to put themselves in places of power; they have avoided these moves and they have been helped in the avoidance by the pressures to keep them out.

At this writing there are only two women in the hundred-seat U.S. Senate. It may be a century more before the makeup of the Senate reflects any real parity between the sexes—not because of a philosophy of gradualism among the women who will lead the change, but because of the way generational patterns influence behavior. Perhaps in two or three generations both sexes will have come to terms with new images of themselves. We are seeing, for example, instances of women bringing their infant children to their places of work, even breast-feeding them there without making their co-workers uncomfortable. And it is not unheard of these days for a man to defer to his wife on the matter of moving to another city for the sake of her career.

So change is evident in a large segment of the population. But there is also confusion and resistance to change. In fact, we are seeing a powerful backlash to the women's movement, an entirely natural reaction. The women's movement has taken an internal pain and externalized it, and this is frightening for many of the women who experience it. Women are being told that they must realize their own potential, yet many know that if they attempt that the edifice of their lives will come tumbling down. They see their friends struggling to change after twenty or thirty years of non-parity with their husbands and they say, "I don't want that struggle, I'd rather be unrealized," and so they choose to stay with the inequality they know, the inequality they can live with. Some who have tried to change have gotten into situations of pressure and responsibility where they feel intensely uncomfortable.

However this may be, I feel that women in our society are more open to change than men, and I believe that this backlash will be temporary. Women will not shrink from the difficult life. Those who are pushing themselves to think, to work, to love, to play to the maximum of their abilities will have more satisfactory lives and will feel better about themselves, however exhausted they may be at the end of their day.

I would remind people not to expect too much of themselves (although this should not be used as an excuse for not trying or for accepting too little). The women's movement has caused pain and engendered anger because it has given people false expectations of their ability to change and because its leaders have often failed to credit the efforts of women—and men—that fall short of the ideal. People coming from very traditional marriages are ill-prepared to have truly equal marriages. They may have to settle for something less. They should struggle together, to move and stretch and reshape, but they shouldn't expect that they can do it all. That's for revolutionaries. Most of us are evolutionaries.

If we have seemed to digress in speaking of the women's-rights movement, it is because this trend bodes well for family life. The family in which each person is accorded his or her rights as a contributing member is an environment that promotes the evolution to maturity. The adolescent will not erupt out of such a system and say good riddance to his family ties. Instead, the doors of the house will open easily at the moment of leaving; the new adult will keep the ties to family in effect while forming new, expanding relationships with equals of both sexes on the outside.

Money and the Family System

The economics of family life—of food, housing, clothing, schooling, medical care—is an issue of such overwhelming importance today that it flavors all family relationships: between husbands and wives, between parents and children. All families have some process for handling these economic questions. Some handle them well, others handle them disastrously.

For example, how do parents go about forming the economic expectations of their children—what will come to them out of the family income in the form of clothes, records, allowances, vacations, and so forth? How is economic support gradually lessened over the child-rearing years, between the time when the child is totally dependent to the time when (you hope) he or she is totally independent? If a teenager has an allowance, how much should it be? When given? Under what circumstances? As the cost of living goes up, should the allowance go up? Is there negotiation on it? Should a working teenager be allowed to keep the money he or she earns? Should they contribute to the family? How much financial help should parents give to their older children without encouraging financial irresponsibility or overindulgence? And when children are financially irresponsible, what might it signify and what can be done?

These and countless other money questions come up in the life of every family. My aim is not to try to answer them specifically, but instead to look at the underlying questions of how money functions in the family system, what rights family members have to a share in their combined income, and how the experiences of past generations affect a family's attitudes toward money. This is important to our subject, because the ability to handle money has much to do with a young person's chances of evolving to emotional maturity and financial independence.

Here again we return to the matter of equality in families.

I believe that the closer a couple or a family can come to the ideal of sharing, the more contentment there will be in that family. In a theoretical family where money is handled well, every person would have knowledge—appropriate to their age—about the family finances and would participate in discussions about how to distribute the assets in accordance with each member's needs. There would be no hidden or nondeclarable income.

It is perhaps shocking to suggest that everyone in a family needs to know about the family's economic position—where the money comes from and how much there is—but this would be closer to life as it was lived in primitive societies, before money appeared and became not so much a means of barter but a way of exercising power. In primitive societies, people had for food and clothing whatever they could kill or hack out of the branches and the earth. They bartered. A drought or a bad harvest or an animal that got away would mean a period of deprivation for everyone. From the time they could reason, children knew these realities of economic life.

In families today money is often a battleground, not because people choose to fight about it but because our society has made it a battleground. Society says that money is the measure of success, and so we advertise our income by how we live, where we live, whom we live next to. Money equals power and control and traditionally, in our patriarchal society, it is the province of the male. All of this is challenged by the idea that families should practice sharing and full disclosure.

Yet I *do* suggest this as the best way to avoid the kind of anger and hostility that follows whenever people in a family get into saying, "This is mine." More than that, sharing should be part of every love relationship where the partners want to be on equal terms and seek the good for each other. Money, once again, is not the issue. The issue has to do with the exercise of power. Nor is this only a man-woman issue. I have seen homosexual couples struggling in the same way to evolve economic equality.

Regardless of the nature of the relationship, I cannot think of a single case where anything but sharing has worked.

Sharing, by this definition, does not mean a precise division. Sharing means simply that everyone in a family deserves a portion of the family income *by reason of being a family member and by fulfilling his or her responsibilities to the family.*

What do I mean by the responsibilities of family members?

In a traditional family, the husband has several responsibilities that are important, but the first one is to provide the sustenance for the family. Again in a traditional family, the wife's basic job is to provide the caretaking of the family—its living and eating arrangements. The children's basic job once they are in school is to go to school and meet the requirements of being a student. Any family member who is doing his or her own job has a right to enjoy some portion of the family income. According to this concept, the mother's piece is due her for taking care of the family; the child's for getting passing grades in school; the husband's for providing bread and shelter. It is not required of the child to do surpassingly well in school, nor is it required of the husband to provide croissants. But if the husband works hard to provide his family with croissants instead of store-bought bread, then that will change the way the family sees him. If the child is at the head of his class, that will influence greatly the way the family looks at the child. If the mother is an excellent cook, that will influence the way the family looks at the mother and treats her. The way the family member performs can go in either direction, but the sharing of the family income should be based on the *completion* of the assigned jobs, not on the quality of the performance. If there isn't completion, then the share should be withheld or renegotiated. There should be as much family discussion as necessary to come to agreement on what each person is responsible for and to fairly distribute the jobs that need doing. If there is no paid help in the house, each of the family members should be responsible for some part of the housework.

Now, if the children are given more jobs than their chief job (getting through school)—if Sarah mows the lawn and Dick tidies the garage—while mother has all the rest of the family jobs and father has only his work to do, there will be an imbalance. An arrangement like that says to the children that everyone has business at home except Dad, that his only business is outside the home. Kids will see and pick up the unfairness of that, and it will serve as a poor model for their future attitudes toward sharing. An even worse model is the situation, so frequent today, where mother works and father works, and even though they both work full time, mother does all the housework.

Although the husband-wife relationship is not specifically the topic of this book—except insofar as it affects the maturation of the children—I would like to say this about the homemaker's share of the family income. It seems reasonable to me that a wife should be paid for her services to the family if that is her major job, just as a husband is paid for his work. One theory of social reform suggests that businesses should issue two checks, one to the husband for the work he does, one to the wife for making it possible for the husband to work. Even if this solution is somewhat farfetched, it is important for husbands and wives to arrive at some arrangement that will keep them on an equal basis, free of the stress caused by an imbalance of power between them.

What we see instead in so many families is that husbands and wives play games about money. They conceal the financial realities from each other. Perhaps the husband gives the wife an allowance, or he has some additional income that he holds back from her. The wife, meanwhile, is squirreling away money because she needs it for things she wants to enjoy but which she feels she can't justify to her husband. Again, this makes a very poor economic model for children to follow and, like all family patterns, it tends to die hard. I believe that when couples quarrel over money it is largely a holdover from their families of origin. The man or the woman, or both, come from parents who had not evolved maturity or equality in discussing economic matters, and they carry this lack of resolution into their own marriages and use economics as their battleground.

Linda and Stan are typical of the couples I see who fight about money. She works in publishing. He is a photographer and he makes about twice as much money as she does. When Stan worked in his studio in their home he used to complain about the money Linda spent having lunch with her friends. Now he's on the staff of a magazine and he, too, is spending money on lunches and drinks with people. I pointed out that this is the same situation in reverse, and questioned why he is not getting mad at himself about it.

Linda and Stan are caught in the traditional model of marriage, where the husband is the breadwinner and likes being the breadwinner, since he feels it gives him the right to tell his wife what to do.

I asked Stan how he would feel if Linda were earning

twice as much income as he does. The idea made him very uncomfortable.

Above and beyond the portion of family income that each member requires to satisfy his or her basic needs, there should be some money to spend with absolutely no strings attached. This, too, is a cost of living; it's the part that makes living fun. If a man goes to the track every Sunday and usually loses money (his wife will greet him on his return by asking, "How much did you lose?" instead of "How did you do?"), the loss can be regarded as a cost of living, not a waste of money. It only gets unfair when the amount spent or lost exceeds the sum set aside for this type of amusement and eats unfairly into the other members' shares of the family income. The "fun fund" is a way of turning a potential conflict that could have detrimental effects on a family into a constructive family pattern whereby each member has some space and wherewithal for personal enjoyment.

First Jobs

When a child starts earning money, he or she moves into an area of family life that in many families is ruled by stereotypical ideas about the handling of money—the right ways and the wrong ways. Kids should be able to feel good and important about earning money. Instead their parents often make them feel as if they were doing something vaguely wrong. That's the message kids get when they hear their parents say, "Put it in the bank," "Don't waste it," "Why are you spending so much on your friends?" "I suppose you're buying pot with it!" and so on.

This question needs to be confronted with clarity, openness, and fairness by all the family members, as in the following example.

Pete is a sophomore in high school who works afternoons and Sundays in a gas station. Between his wage (the minimum) and tips, he's making about eighty dollars a week. His father is an accountant in a small firm, with an income of about five hundred dollars a week. Pete's mother works mornings as a doctor's receptionist, which brings another one hundred dollars weekly into the family pot. What with car and mortgage payments, food, and other expenses, Pete's parents are spending every penny they make just to keep the household afloat. They think Pete should contribute something too, a fixed weekly sum. Is this a fair request?

We are proposing that the money a family makes should be regarded as family income and that everybody in the family has some right to the income, based on their contribution as family members. As things are in *this* family, Pete's father doesn't really own his five hundred dollars a week, nor does his mother own her one hundred dollars a week, so it would hardly be fair if Pete owned his eighty dollars a week.

Should Pete have anything of what he earns free and unencumbered, or should it all be added to the family cake and reapportioned back to him as one of a family of four? Should Pete's eighty dollars a week make the difference as to whether his kid sister gets to go to the movies on Saturday afternoons?

Pete's family has to negotiate this matter based on the needs of each member and on how much of each person's responsibility is fulfilled by the dollars they bring in.

If the family absolutely needed Pete's eighty dollars to get by, then it would be part of the family income and represent Pete's contribution to the survival of the family. But this is not the case here. Pete's parents are meeting their obligations out of their own earnings. Moreover, Pete's job is something he does over and above his other responsibilities to the family (his jobs at home include taking care of his mother's car for her, and at school he is getting scholarship grades). Pete might contribute by paying for his clothes and incidental expenses. And if he does that, it would be fair for him to "own" his eighty dollars, except for perhaps some small weekly contribution to the household expenses.

If we were to revisit Pete some years later and find him working full time and making a decent salary but still living at home, the same guidelines would apply about contributing to the family income. At this point, he is still a family member but his place is less central to the system. He is thinking of starting a family of his own and the hours he spends at home are little more than the hours of eating and sleeping. He no longer has the responsibility of school work, and although he still takes care of his mother's car, he also uses it to take his girl friend out on dates. At this time, Pete, for whom home is becoming more like a boardinghouse, could be asked to give an increased contribution to the running of the household.

Later, when Pete marries and moves out of his parents' house, then his financial responsibility will be toward his new family.

The Financially Irresponsible Child

The family we have been describing is one with fairly straightforward money problems. The son always knew the financial score in his home and was party to the family effort to achieve a comfortable life for all, and largely in consequence of this he learned to handle money well.

Other households present a different picture. I am think-ing, for example, of Kim, a chronic check-bouncer, whose very well-to-do family is constantly coming to her aid and putting money into her account. I am thinking, too, of John, a young man who runs up his charge card accounts to the point where he is hopelessly in debt and then *his* fairly well-to-do parents have to step in and bail him out.

Money has a special meaning for these young people. It seems to function as a reminder of their parents' love for them, since it brings their parents running to their rescue. Finding a way to discontinue this pattern would mean changing the systemic operation that brought it about—no easy matter.

In this kind of situation, parents often try the obvious cure: disassociating themselves from their child's way-wardness. ("This is the last time, John. If you get in over your head again, don't come to us, we won't help you.")

Why does this approach so often fail? Perhaps because it goes against my axiom that all behaviors are attempts to save the family, not to destroy it. The children will go on needing the financial crutch and the parents will go on holding it out to them, until some other way is found to convey the love that the money represents.

If we Think the Unthinkable in this matter, one solution that comes to mind is for the family to make frequent and large enough gifts of money to their child so that it would be impossible for him or her to overspend. Of course, this might bankrupt the family, but the idea is no more unreal-istic than a "solution" that withdraws the help and offers nothing in its place.

Here is a solution worked out by one family as the fairest way of resolving what had become a painful situa-tion for them all. It is a letter of agreement written in legal

terms but not intended to be legally binding. It reads as
follows:

QUASI-LEGAL DOCUMENT

BE IT KNOWN TO ALL THREE UNDERSIGNED THAT
A) AFTER JANUARY 31, 1981, JOHN JONES AND JANE
   JONES WILL NO LONGER HONOR THE DEBTS OF AND/OR
   EXPENSES INCURRED BY THEIR SON JOHN JONES, JR.:
B) THE AMOUNT TO BE PAID TO JOHN JONES, JR., IN
   SETTLEMENT OF HIS DEBTS BEFORE THE END OF
   JANUARY 1981 SHALL BE AS LITTLE AS POSSIBLE:
C) FROM FEBRUARY 1, 1981, AND FORWARD JOHN JONES,
   JR., WILL BE SOLELY AND EXCLUSIVELY RESPONSIBLE
   FOR FINANCIALLY MAINTAINING HIMSELF ACCORDING
   TO THE MONETARY MEANS (HIS SALARY) AVAILABLE
   TO HIM.
SIGNED IN THE FERVENT AND SINCERE HOPE THAT THEIR
OTHERWISE WONDERFUL SON WILL SUCCEED IN RIDDING HIM-
SELF OF THIS PLAGUE THAT WE AND SOCIETY HAVE SOMEHOW
PUT UPON HIM AND THAT WE SHALL SET HIM FREE, NOT EVER
FROM OUR LOVE, BUT FROM OUR KEEPING.

_____   _____
JOHN JONES   DATE

_____   _____
JANE JONES   DATE

SIGNED IN AGREEMENT WITH THE ABOVE, RECOGNIZING THAT
THE TASK AHEAD IS DIFFICULT BUT CERTAIN OF MY DESIRE TO
BUILD A PRODUCTIVE AND SATISFYING LIFE OF MY OWN,
INDEPENDENT OF MY PARENTS' AUTHORITY BUT NEVER WITHOUT
THEIR LOVE AND AFFECTION.

_____   _____
JOHN JONES, JR.   DATE

Here, of course, the parents are withdrawing financial
aid, but in such a way that they affirm their love for and

confidence in their child, while he is able to affirm his respect for his parents and his desire to take responsibility for his own life.

Riches, it seems, are not necessarily liberating for a family. For example, a parent who is earning an astronomical salary in industry is likely to have some guilt about making so much money. He becomes secretive about how much money is actually there, and because of his feelings he finds it difficult to set limits on how much he gives his children; in his striving to do the best for his family he does the absolute worst. A typical pattern is for the parent to dole out the money to a child in varying sums. Unfortunately, the sums tend to get bigger as the child spends more and runs up bigger debts, and smaller as the child is better behaved. (Our society operates in much the same way in certain sectors. For example, it does not reward families for remaining intact; its welfare laws actually encourage the breakup of families.) How is a child to evolve maturity if his negative behaviors are rewarded and his positive behaviors are not?

Money need not be such a murderous thing to handle. Many families handle it for the benefit of all. And from what I have seen, I would say that the key to this approach is equality of information about fiscal matters in the family. There should be no secrets. Parents should deal from the realities of the situation and not be ashamed about having money—if indeed they have it. The closer families can come to this openness, the easier it will be for their children to handle financial matters.

I recall, when I was a young man in the army, visiting a friend of mine and his wife in their very cramped and sparsely furnished apartment. Three blocks away his father and mother lived in a magnificent house. At the time I felt outraged on my friend's behalf at this inequity. Now I would be more inclined to credit his parents for living on the level of comfort and enjoyment that their wealth made possible at that time in their lives. I am reminded of this family because they illustrate a second principle for helping offspring learn to live with and understand money, that is, the acknowledgment of appropriate limits. Equal knowledge of family income does not mean equal distribution of money. In the hierarchical structure of the family, the child who fulfills his family responsibility has a right to a share in the family income proportionate to his or her place in the hierarchy. Although children are full members of the family, they are not automatically the equals of their parents.

This hierarchy is a changing one, however, and as a child grows so do his needs and responsibilities and ways of sharing. The status of the infant at his mother's breast is entirely different from the status of his sixteen-year-old brother; that child not only needs and wants food (but only of a particular kind—mostly junk), but also a room of his own with a padlocked door six inches thick for the times he needs privacy.

At all stages in life, the thing that children need most from their family is not money, however. It is the security of knowing that they are loved and respected and that they are responsible members of their family. This is what gives them strength to face the world as they try to evolve their adult identities.

8

TROUBLED FAMILIES

Most of us parents have some family we know that we look on as a model of perfection or near-perfection. Perhaps the children were outstanding in high school, went on to prestigious colleges, graduated with honors, appear to have perfect relationships with their parents, their peers, and their institutions. We look at ourselves and see that we've been in a benevolent state of war with our own children at least since the time they were teenagers, and it makes us wonder if there isn't something terribly wrong.

It might help if we knew that the perfect family—the one whose members enjoy a constant state of ease and comfort with each other—is a mythical family. True, some families function better than others and some function very well indeed, but the family itself is a construct that must sometimes be dis-eased and discontented (in the sense we explained earlier) *as part of the normal continuum of life.*

If we could know that model family intimately enough, we would find enough dis-ease in their lives to make us feel better about our own family. The "perfect family" is likely to be the one whose members are less ready to share their

A *family member's seemingly disruptive behaviors are not "bad" behaviors. Rather, they are the behaviors the family has available to it at that time for maintaining homeostasis.*

family traumas, less free to bring out from the back reaches of their minds the problems that remain unresolved.

"Normal" and "Abnormal" Families

Families do differ from one another, but not in the sense that some are "normal" and others are "abnormal." We prefer to think of a family's behavior as coming somewhere on a spectrum defined at one end by families who feel themselves to be deeply troubled and at the other end by families who feel themselves to be relatively trouble-free. The emotional basis of behavior is the same across the spectrum, but in troubled families the expression of emotion is carried to extreme lengths. For example, all children are violent to a degree, or angry to a degree, or destructive to a degree, or sloppy or dirty or whatever *to a degree*, and some individuals within that great mass exhibit those qualities in more extreme ways. Consider how many people at times say or feel, "I could kill him" and fortunately how seldom anyone carries that anger to its most extreme expression—murder.

Even for health professionals, it often takes close observation to differentiate a family that is in trouble from a family that is functioning well. Some families seem bizarre in their life-styles, yet they function with resiliency and are fully accepted by society.

One important key to good functioning in families seems to be the way they cope with stress. For example, when one member of a so-called normal family has a chronic disease, the family will investigate every way of dealing with the illness; the generations will cooperate and be supportive of the sick member, and this becomes a matter of course in their lives, not a source of friction.

In the family that cannot cope well, the illness seems to crowd out other activities and exacerbates other difficulties that may exist. If there is unhappiness or unfairness or failure to communicate in that family, it is likely to be blamed on the illness. In some cases, the illness seems to fill a family need. (A family in which the forty-five-year-old unmarried son had a stroke recognized this vaguely when they said, "One thing about the stroke, it's gotten us back together again.")

Often, a very troubled family may single out one problem to focus on without having any true sense of what their real problems are. I recall a family of five who had among them severe problems of chronic disease and mental disturbance and who came to therapy not for those reasons but because the school marks of one of the children had fallen from B to C minus.

Society cannot really be the judge as to which families are in need of help. What society can do is to offer help to families when their perceptions of themselves or their feelings tell them that they are in trouble. The help that is offered should treat the problem as one affecting the system rather than a single individual in the system.

In families where there are young adults, two common problems are depression and various forms of antisocial behavior. There are many other problems, of course, but we will concentrate here on these two areas in order to illustrate some of the kinds of difficulty that can be helped by family-systems therapy. We do not look at any one problem in terms of isolated facts ("Why did Johnny break into the gas station at two o'clock in the morning?"), but rather we look at it as a systemic manifestation ("What did Johnny's act mean in the operation of that family system?").

Whatever the problem, the question to be answered is,

How is the system working? What is really happening there? What are the balances and how do they fit? We say that everything in the situation has a function. (Theoretically, if we could arrive at a perfect understanding of a situation and translate it into a mechanical model, the pluses and minuses would balance each other out; we would be able to see exactly how the family system works and keeps itself in balance.)

As it is, family therapists have to work backward, in a sense. We begin with the premise that families always maintain their homeostasis, and in each particular situation we try to see how the dynamics of the family are operating to incorporate all changes. How the problem will be treated depends on the therapist; approaches vary. But the basic question—what is really happening there?—has to be answered first.

The "whys" ("Why is Johnny doing this?") that family members so often voice in connection with their problems, discomfort, and misery often presuppose some destructive motive on the part of the troublesome family member. Let me repeat a point made in chapter 1, namely, that family members always do what they do in order to keep the family unchanged and safe. Often, society and the family look on an individual member's behavior as antithetical to family harmony.

Nevertheless, if that aforementioned mechanical model could be built into the situation, taking every aspect into account, it would show how the move served to keep the *status quo*, to keep the family in balance. Consider, for example, a child who causes his recently divorced parents to come together over the problem of his misbehavior in school; by making trouble he is accomplishing something he can do in no other way—getting his parents together.

This is, of course, a very simple and obvious example of

trying to hold the system together, but it illustrates how so-called self-defeating behaviors are actually *systemic self-maintaining* behaviors. In a system, the individual acts not as a "self" but as a part of the system, influencing all the other parts and being influenced by them.

Depression in Young Adults

Depressed young people may appear to their parents to be inert, unresponsive, indolent, fearful of the outside world, perhaps exploitive of their parents' protectiveness. The kinds of things the family may do to help in these situations—commonsense moves like pressuring the child to act, sending him or her to a psychiatrist or therapist—may actually worsen the situation. What, then, can families do to help a child get over his or her depression?

I would say first that I think it is a normal part of life for people to go through periods of depression. More than that, periods of depression serve a very valuable function in making us aware of the difference between feeling happy and feeling sad. If we didn't experience the contrast between the two emotions, our periods of happiness would be meaningless. (Similarly, people who are psychotic have moments or periods of sanity, which is how they know they are insane—and they always know they are insane. Perhaps the basic difference between sane people and insane people is that the latter suffer longer periods of dis-ease in comparison with "sane" people, who have their dis-ease under better control. The dis-ease of the sane is societally functional; the dis-ease of the insane is societally nonfunctional.)

If, then, we need periods of thoughtfulness and sadness, we should come to accept them as part of our totality. If, as it seems, there must always be some area in our lives of incompleteness or poor functioning, then we must learn to live at peace with our imperfectability.

The point of what I am saying is this: in trying to deal with the depression of one member, a family should try not to get depressed about the depression. If they accept that life has both good times and bad times, they will be less likely to react with panic, anger, or shame. This is what happens in many families, and it sometimes becomes more of a problem than the depression itself.

Often, in their efforts to help a deeply depressed child, the family puts the child into therapy with a psychiatrist, psychoanalyst, psychologist, or other mental health professional. Whatever the indications for and possible benefits of this move, it also identifies the child to himself and others as troubled, as someone inferior, and thus it adds another layer to the cover of family problems that already exist. Not infrequently, patients come to family-systems therapy who have spent thousands of hours and many more thousands of dollars in individual therapy without being able to get free of their rage or depression or whatever it is that imprisons them.

As long as the young person is still centrally located in his family system, the treatment for depression should be one that takes the system into account. I do not discount the classical treatments for depression, or the promising new drug therapies, but if the treatment doesn't also examine and treat the systemic stresses, can we reasonably expect the depression to go away?

What a depressed young person needs is not pressure to perform; that will only alienate him further from his family, his peers, and himself. He needs to be helped to feel as good as he can about himself, to be more secure, more confident in his abilities, so that his fears of going into the world will be lessened. He should not be confronted but should be engaged in a side-by-side consideration of his problems; he himself may be the best guide in finding the moves that can help bring this about. The family should fasten on whatever progress he makes, however tiny, not on his errors or shortcomings or inertia.

In treating depression, it is easy to concentrate on the problems of the individual while giving too little thought to the cultural and environmental aspects. A depressed person has trouble letting his energies flow into various forms of activity: the energy is there, but it gets short-circuited. This is likely to happen in families where there is little zest for living and few activities where energy can surface and find expression. This, I think, is partly a problem of our society. We tend to be overly serious and to assign our times of joyous celebration to certain prescribed holidays or family occasions. We've largely gotten away from the old-world customs of eating and drinking and playing heartily as a matter of everyday life. I think some of this has to do with the Puritan ethic, which tells us to work hard and spend the night sleeping, and not to laugh too much or tell too many jokes (and certainly no dirty ones). The effects of this can be seen in the world around us. Some families seem to discount the fun times; ask them what happens in their lives and they report only troubles and unhappiness. As you walk along the street, notice how few of the people seem to be having a good time. If you go to a film comedy notice how the audience seems to take its cue from the two or three people among them who are really enjoying themselves. In the bars and restaurants where young people meet, you will find plenty of animation and high-pitched talk but rarely a belly laugh, and when someone does laugh that way it draws looks of disdain, as if the laughing person were crazy.

Fun is difficult to deal with also because there is an element of violence in every belly laugh. To have real humor means being willing to let go, to take a chance. That's why it's easier to keep the lid on humor. We all know people we might call "even-keelers"; they want their boat always to be in balance, not to dip or heel to one side or the other. Their lives are remarkable for the absence of crests and troughs, triumphs and defeats.

I must admit that I cannot say whether a family should even-keel through life or whether it should brave the open sea. But I do believe that a family that lives with zest, that is available to experience, that is not afraid of the kind of energy that finds expression in humor, is a family that is less prone to depression.

The family is a safe place where we can be ourselves. No one else knows us as well, nowhere else do we have the kind of trust we share with other family members. The family is the logical arena for fun, and perhaps one day our culture will get back to the custom of family get-togethers where a kind of relating goes on that cannot happen among strangers—or among people who have no family ties.

Runaways

One of the saddest, most painful events that can occur in family life is when a teenager runs away from home, not out of a taste for adventure or precocious readiness for life but out of loneliness and the sense of being an outsider in his or her own home.

The terrible bind of the runaway was brought home to me several years ago when I worked with homeless children in New York's Greenwich Village. These young people had an intense desire to be connected, but they were convinced that they were not wanted at home and would

not be allowed back even if they went home. As is true in
general of runaways, they had very low self-esteem; they
saw themselves as total negatives, and when they connected with other runaways—as is the tendency—they had
their negatives reinforced. Many were clearly on paths that
would lead to early death.

Such was the case with one young man whose name was
Harold. When I first met him, he was about seventeen,
sandy-haired, nice-looking, somewhat thin but well built
and possessed of a very engaging manner. He seemed easy
to communicate with, and, being inexperienced at the
time, I thought I would have little trouble helping him. I
spent hours talking with him and learned that he liked to
get a high from drinking cough medicine containing codeine, as much as eight bottles of it a day.

As Harold grew to trust me, he became more confiding.
He told me how bad things had been at home before he
went away and how the codeine had helped him handle
his life. After several weeks he finally told me who his parents were and where they lived. I asked Harold if he would
let me call them. "No, no," he said, "don't call them, because they don't want me home anymore." Occasionally
after that, I brought the matter up again; I was certain because of the ease with which Harold related to me that he
had some desire to talk with an adult person and that he
might be ready to be less alone in the world. Finally he allowed me to call his parents, who lived in southern New
Jersey.

His father answered the phone, and what I heard in his
voice was not relief or eagerness to see his son, but instead
a great reluctance to come and meet Harold. "Just send
him home," he said.

I said, "At the moment Harold is fearful about coming
home."

"Fearful of what?" he asked touchily.

I said, "He feels that he's been a failure and that he's better off away and that the family's better off without him."

Harold's father said, "Well, he was very difficult to get along with while he was here. He was doing drugs. He'd come home high all the time. We couldn't talk to him at all. Probably I couldn't talk to him now any better. Suppose you put him on the phone and let me talk to him."

I asked Harold to come and talk to his father but he was shaking with fear and wouldn't come to the phone.

I ended the conversation with his father and tried to talk to Harold about going home. If anything, the chasm in his mind separating him from his parents had been widened rather than narrowed by the phone contact. His thought processes were confused, probably due to his drug-taking, and it was difficult to get him to concentrate. No matter what I did after that, I was unable to get the son and the father to come toward each other. Both seemed afraid to make that move.

A few weeks after the call, Harold suddenly disappeared and he never returned while I was at the agency. Some years later, I heard that he had died from his codeine addiction.

The act of running away is a powerful systemic move. It leaves a big hole in the family. In a sense it is a sacrificial act, an attempt to change what is uncomfortable, and it does—it must—bring about change, though not necessarily a change in the right direction. How much better if a family could change without this drastic move!

Harsh measures are not the answer to keeping a runaway at home (they are rarely a solution to any problem). Rather, parents need to find ways to reduce the discomfort and pressure that caused the child to leave, just as they might take steps to bring a high fever down into the normal range.

The runaway needs first and foremost to be made comfortable, to be made to feel that he belongs and is wanted. Just as you might soothe a feverish child with an alcohol bath, you can do things for the runaway that have the effect of reducing pressure. You might buy him some new clothes of the kind *he* likes, cook the kinds of food *he* enjoys, make an occasional present of something *he* wants. Once a certain level of communication is reached through loving gestures, the parents should try to share *their* feelings with the child. The runaway needs to hear his parents say how much they missed him, how things were worse without him rather than better, how the void created by his leaving was far more painful to them than any of his troublesome behavior.

I know that what I suggest is very difficult to do; the very fact of the running-away is a sign that a family is having trouble relating comfortably. Indeed, in many families a child's running-away becomes a life pattern and the parents become almost used to it. Some parents may even come to feel that the child's life will be better "out there," since he or she was so uncomfortable and unhappy at home. It is a kind of sad and mistaken benevolence, with each side hoping that the life of the other will be better because of the separation. It really isn't callousness when parents say, "What are we coming together for? If we do, nothing will be different. We're all going to be as unhappy as we were before." It is the only way they can see at that moment to do what seems best for the family.

If a family is not able to help itself, and if it cannot bring about the necessary reduction of pressure, then a doctor or therapist should be called in to help it find ways to keep the child home. Losing a child, if only briefly, to the cruel subculture of the runaways is too great a price to pay for accomplishing systemic change.

No resolution of relationships is possible for the young person who runs away and stays away. The family will always be a force in his life, something he seeks in other disguises. The connections he makes, even if they are positive, cannot bring real peace; this is possible only when he is securely connected with his family of origin.

Drug-Taking

In the matter of drugs, the reality of life in our present culture is that drugs of every sort are available to young people. In this country we label drugs as illicit and give lip service to our abhorrence of drug use, but the truth is we have given drugs an important place in our national life. Drugs are on the campuses, in the offices, at dinner parties, at beer busts, in the family medicine cabinet. The sources for them exist and those who are intent on using drugs learn how to find those sources; often the sellers come to them. Indeed, you would be hard put to find a young person who hasn't had to say yes or no to the offer of some kind of drug either from a friend or from a pusher.

It is this situation, and not any tendency to condone, that leads me to say, as I do in chapter 2, that it is the norm for young people today to engage in a certain amount of experimentation with drugs and alcohol. I return to the topic here since, obviously, a great many young people go beyond the "norm"—as Harold did—and get into a dependency on drugs that blights and perhaps even destroys their lives.

The way families handle the drug-taking has much to do with the eventual outcome. Suppose we imagine two families, similar in their social status and makeup, of which each has a child who is a fairly heavy user of drugs. In the first family, the Browns, the members are able to name the problem, to take positions, and to feel it as a source of dis-ease in the family, for which they try to find solutions. The Smith family, on the other hand, operates in such a way that even though their child has deteriorated physically and is plainly showing the effects of the drug use, the members have no forum for bringing the problem into the open. Homeostasis for them means incorporating the problem into their life, as if their child's drug-taking were a normal behavior.

In a family like the Browns, the outlook is much more favorable. When a youngster sees in his family a serious but not hysterical concern about his problem with drugs, he is likely to discontinue the drug-taking as he gets older or to treat it as a fairly innocuous occasional indulgence. But a youngster in a family like the Smiths is likely to be in deeper trouble. That family might not be able to look at the problem until they are forced to by the child's taking an overdose or getting into some kind of trouble with the law.

The difference between these two families, as regards drugs, lies in the ability of the first to deal with the reality of the drug problem in their midst. Their sense of dis-ease leads them to take the necessary steps—perhaps even to seek outside help in the form of family therapy. Families of the latter type come for help—if they do at all—at a much more advanced and difficult stage of the problem.

The conclusion I have come to out of my experience with young people is that the elaborate system we have constructed to safeguard Americans against drugs actually works in the opposite direction. I believe it tends to foster the use of drugs in our population. There is, in the first place, the immense amount of money to be made in dealing with something illicit and therefore "hard to get." It means that kids who want to buy drugs must come into contact with the people and the workings of the underworld, an experience that may be more damaging to them than the drugs themselves. Or, they succumb to the lure of the money and start dealing themselves. Moreover, the very illicitness of drugs makes drug-taking an obvious area of adolescent testing.

The expense to society of drug prohibition is far beyond anything we can imagine, and despite all the money and time spent—on cloak-and-dagger operations to break up drug rings, on control procedures (counting pills) in pharmaceutical houses and hospital stockrooms, on crop-dusting flights over marijuana fields, and the like—still the drugs are there for those who want them.

It is my hope that somehow in the future this nation will find a way to make drugs legally available and that it will spend some of the money saved on community services to help substance abusers and their families. Legalization, I'm sure, will bring its own problems, but I believe it will make possible more realistic and effectual efforts to combat drug addiction.

Stealing and Vandalism

Whatever social environment a family belongs to—from the ghetto to the most exclusive and wealthy community—there seems to be no guarantee that its children will not engage at one time or another in antisocial behavior, including vandalism and stealing. Every community has its stories to tell: of houses broken into and wantonly trashed; of money, jewelry, TV sets, and even automobiles taken by young people who may be the friends—even the children—

of the victims. The shame and bewilderment of the parents, as well as the embarrassment of their friends and neighbors, make it seem better to play down these acts, to make allowances for the young people rather than come to grips with the problem of why they do these things and where it will lead them.

It is a mistake, I believe, not to deal seriously with behavior of this kind. I am not speaking of the kind of stealing that small children do during the five- to eight-year-old period. It is not unusual for a child of that age to take small things, and it is usually enough for the parents to tell the child that stealing is unacceptable, to make the incident into a simple object lesson. However, when teenagers engage in stealing and serious vandalism, it's time to consider getting outside help to deal with the problem. It is unrealistic to brush off such behavior in the belief that it will cure itself, like adolescent acne.

Parents of law-breaking young people often say, "It's that crowd he runs around with that gets him in trouble."

Blaming the child's peers may make the parents feel better, but the peers are really a red herring. The blame does not rest there. Within the child's group, there are some kids who stay on the sidelines when it comes to these activities, or if they do get involved, they manage not to get caught. No one in the group is actually compelled to engage in troublemaking.

It is not a random thing that some young people engage in antisocial behavior while others do not. If we could know intimately all the families of troublemaking children, we would discover the reasons why the kids do what they do. So long as families look *outside* themselves for the reasons why things happen, they will not be able to get at the realities of their situation.

Take, for example, a very poor family that is kept in a

state of high anxiety by the delinquent behavior of an adolescent child. It may be that by being so involved with the delinquent behavior, the parents have no time to look at the abjectness of their own existence. Unconsciously the child sees that his behavior takes his parents' attention off their own situation and he knows no other way to do this. If the child does things that cause him to be put into jail or into a home for delinquents, he may be unconsciously motivated by the need to remove a sore (himself) from their existence, perhaps to make life easier for a family that is having enough trouble, he thinks, just putting food on the table. Which of us hasn't heard some youngster say that his family would be better off without him?

A family does not need to be poor to experience this kind of diversionary behavior on the part of the child. Often a child's antisocial behavior goes along with tension in the family on other issues, sometimes a failure of the parents to resolve a problem in their own relationship.

Stealing as a behavior has extreme connotations. It is a call for attention, a cry for help. If a young person is not stealing to subsist, then it is an indication of a breakdown, a feeling of disconnection in his life.

I have seen it happen in families that a child gets into petty break-ins or some such activity during a time when his parents are having a very rocky period in their marriage. But when the parents—either through counseling or by other means—settle their differences and remove this stress, the child does not always stop the stealing.

This continuing behavior may relate to "unfinished business" in the system that has re-formed as a result of marriage counseling or divorce; the parents have not yet established clear lines of responsibility in their changed relationship, which the child needs in order to help him break the pattern he got into during the time of great stress.

In chapter 6 we spoke about the need for re-formation after a family goes through divorce or change following marital separation. This is the kind of problem where that need is painfully demonstrated.

When a child of wealthy parents turns to stealing, it may signal a crisis in values. Money in the family may be as plentiful as leaves on the trees and just as lightly disposed of. The parents may be giving out to the world the message that they can buy anything, go anywhere, live in a half-dozen places, and yet they say to their child, "You can have only so much allowance. You have to draw the line on the clothes you want [or the trips, or equipment, or whatever]." The child feels restricted, and so he "borrows" in order to redress the imbalance between himself and his parents.

It is certainly necessary to place limits on the funds available to a child (as we pointed out in the previous chapter), but the problem here is the seeming hypocrisy of parents like these, since they apply no limitation to themselves in the use of money and yet they expect a conservative attitude toward money from their child.

When a young person gets his name on the police blotter for a prank or a minor illegal activity of some kind, the matter should not be blown out of proportion. But if a pattern of incidents develops, the family is doing the child a disservice if it tries to gloss over the problem. This is to turn a deaf ear to what might be a child's call for help. One possible course of action is to seek professional help *as a family*. The therapist who is chosen should be able to meet with the entire family at one time—at least initially—

and to have the cooperation of everyone in addressing the problem.

Bringing About Family Change

In describing the process of change in families, we might take the familiar image of the square peg in the square hole. If we change the shape of the peg so that it is eight-sided, we also have to change the shape of the hole, or the peg won't fit. What makes change in families so difficult is that the "fit" becomes firmly established. Everything in the system is functionally there; everything—even trouble—somehow works in balancing the system, and if anything in the system changes, then the system has to find a way to refit and rebalance.

As we said earlier, when families start to change, they find it hard to get comfortable with the differences. They are experts at handling the trouble they know. The depressed person may learn to smile, but if he finds himself smiling too often he feels guilty about it and may return to the more "comfortable" state of being depressed. A person who feels guilty about having money may manage to stay poor or else find ways to "pay" for his successes. The person whose life has been a series of troubles may continue to go from crisis to crisis, handling them, because this is what he does well; normally he will avoid making the choices that would lead to a safe, secure existence. The person who is moved into a job that confers new power and prestige may be gripped with fear, despite having the skills and ability for the job.

Change in an established pattern can only come about in tiny increments, because the system cannot absorb and integrate any drastic, sudden differences. Frequently, when

families attempt sudden changes, they find out after their
efforts are spent that nothing has changed. (Dieting offers
an example. Almost anyone who has ever been successful
at losing considerable weight and keeping it off has learned
that it cannot be done through crash dieting, but only by
systemic change—learning to think differently about food,
putting different kinds and amounts of food on the table,
using it differently in social situations, learning to appreciate it rather than gulping it down.)

Anyone who wishes to change has to come to grips with
the fear that accompanies change, has to be able to recognize the fear in operation and not give up the effort. The
problem is not that there aren't choices of other ways to
go; nor do we lack the imagination to think of them if we
really try. The problem is that it is monumentally difficult
to take one of these choices and work on it while resisting
the pressures the system exerts to keep us in the old, established ways.

Even the physical self sometimes enters the battle to
keep the system from changing. Headaches, dizziness, and
ulcers that act up are just a few of the ways the body responds to the discomfort sometimes engendered when we
try to do things differently. I have seen this at work in my
own life, most recently when I was faced with an important career change. There was no other stress that I could
point to in my life at the time, yet despite this knowledge I
was having to take medicine for a variety of (I hope) transitory physical ills. It was a humbling experience for someone whose profession is to help people change, and all I
could do was worry and try to laugh about it and wait for
the differences to be integrated in my life.

So far we have been discussing the subject of change in
families without particular reference to the parenting of
young adults. This is because change is systemic and in-

volves everyone in the family. By way of illustration, suppose we look at a family whose teenage son, Scotty, is frequently in trouble—with his parents, with authorities at school, and on one or two occasions, with the police.

Scott could be thought of as an outright bad student or an outright "bad boy," but he is neither of these things. He is a combination of many things. He is sometimes straightforward and sometimes circuitous. He is sometimes serious at school, but mostly he doesn't seem to care. He is sometimes responsible and sometimes flagrantly irresponsible. When he tries to be truthful, no one believes him because they can't tell whether he is telling the truth or lying. By now his pattern of erratic behavior is firmly entrenched in the minds of his family. He senses in them the expectation that it's only a matter of time before he'll be back in trouble. So the pattern is transmitted—from him to them, from them back to him—and their expectations only reinforce the likelihood that he will err again.

What makes Scotty's case more complicated is that he still seems to try at times to do better. But the moves he makes to raise the level of his family's esteem for him by doing well are not sufficient to outweigh his negative moves. His parents can't accept what he does well (getting mostly passing grades at midterm) because they are so absorbed in what he does badly (leaving a New Year's Eve party in a car that didn't belong to him and getting into an accident with it). Scott's progress is in loops: an up side followed by a down side, and the down side influences the way his family views his accomplishments. His mother may say, "Well, look, he did get passing grades," and his father says, "That's only because we got him a lot of help."

It is immensely difficult to break a pattern like this, to find ways that haven't already been tried and defeated by the family system. Rewards, limitations, and encouragements that are tried are likely to be swallowed and disappear as if they'd been cast into quicksand.

The most helpful thing a family can do to change this kind of backsliding problem is to try to fasten on the positives, to react in ways that give credit for whatever degree of progress has been made. If parents and others in authority can do this, it is likely that the progress will eventually outstrip the backsliding.

Families can change if they persevere in the effort, despite their painfully slow progress, and not revert to where they were before. They must give change a chance, give the system time to relevel itself after each new input.

The Role of the Therapist

Often, what starts the process of change in families is a crisis—an unusually painful event or an intolerable level of emotional stress. Some families, in their efforts to survive a crisis, seek help through family-systems therapy.

Family therapy is an approach that works in the full frame of the family system. Using forces already at work in the system, it tries to help family members alter their pattern of interdependency and get free of their enmeshment. A time of crisis that shakes the family up may be felt by the family as painful, but it also opens up possibilities for new courses of action. The therapist tries to help family members through their crisis, not just by taking away the pain but by acting as a guide and resourcer to possible new ways of living in relation to one another.

The process of family-systems therapy involves more than counseling and encouragement. The therapist literally enters the system, and the addition of the new "member" forces change in the way the members interact with each

other and with the therapist, so that the system necessarily
has to rebalance itself.

This therapy works on the belief that *every* behavior has
a function in maintaining the family system. But in order
to find out what the function of a particular behavior is,
the therapist needs to see and understand *everything* that
is going on in the family. That is why family therapists
often decline cases where the whole family refuses to come
in, at least initially, as a group. Only when parents, siblings, and all other involved persons come together at once
is it possible to see fully and understand what is happening. The "why" will become evident when the "what" is
discovered.

Perhaps the hardest part of the therapist's job is depriv-
ing the family of the idea that one or more of its members
are responsible for its problems. Blame is not possible or
acceptable in the systemic approach, because it is the system, not the self, that creates the situation. Like guilt,
blaming is something we use to avoid coming to grips with
our problems. For example, if a therapist is dealing with a
family that includes a sick child, the family may point to
the sickness as the cause of its discomfort. But the therapist does not proceed only by treating the child. Instead,
he treats a family that, as a whole, has an illness. Another
family may have that same illness in one of its members
and be able to cope with it quite well. With the former
family, the illness may be the catalyst that brings them to
therapy; their real problem is something far more complicated, of which their inability to cope with the illness is
symptomatic.

Among its goals, family-systems therapy seeks to prevent
the isolation of troubled persons—in their illness, in their
insanity, in their deviant behavior, or in some other painful
difficulty. Isolation can be particularly tragic in cases of

mental illness, which is so often related to unresolved family relationships and is so often treated by cutting the individual off from his or her family in order to undergo institutional treatment. In the systemic approach, there is no such thing as a mentally ill individual, only systems in which mental illness is operating.

Family therapists do suggest moves they hope will bring about change in family behavior, and sometimes these moves are both difficult and startling. At all times they should be moves that the system is ready for. For example, I once ordered a couple to stop their constant fighting. And for a week they did stop. When I said to them, "That's pretty silly, that you stopped fighting just because I said so," they replied, "Well, it's what we needed to hear." What happened, I believe, is that the ground for this move was prepared and they could act on something that came from me because they felt the correctness of the move and because I had positioned myself in the system in such a way that they could hear it from me. I substituted peace for fighting and they were ready to find out what peace felt like.

A far more difficult move seemed necessary in the case of the Torres family. The marriage of the parents was ready to break up, and the household was in a state of constant tension because of the behavior of the seventeen-year-old son, Phil, who was the eldest of the three children, all boys. Phil flunked out of school, made promises he didn't fulfill, refused to work, and made a mess of the house. Testing indicated that he was minimally brain-damaged. After many unsuccessful attempts at bringing order into Phil's life and the life of his family, it seemed to me and the parents that the only course of action open to them was to lock Phil out of the house. And his parents did lock him out.

Persevering in this course of action proved harrowing for us all. Phil was angry and accusing toward his parents. He flirted with the world of drugs; he pleaded with neighbors and social agencies to get his parents to relent. I would receive calls from various well-meaning agencies saying, "Mr. Maslow, we have to get a hold of Philip's parents, this is terrible, he needs them badly. We've got to get them over here and interview them." And I would say, "No, no, do whatever you can for him. Give him food, give him therapy, give him shelter, but as far as his parents are concerned, if Phil wants to reach them he knows how, and if he wants to reach me he knows how."

After about six months, parents and son were genuinely missing each other. Phil told his parents that he was willing to change and they let him come home temporarily to live. He found a job and showed considerable improvement in his social behavior. His parents, who had worked together to strengthen their marriage, felt better about their relationship and better about themselves. They had answered the question of whether they really wanted to change, and whether they could stand the change of letting Phil take responsibility for himself. The effect of the move was to put Phil's progress in his hands and his parents' progress in their hands.

I did not take away the trouble of this family, and I didn't help their troubled son to become maximally functioning. But I did help them all to see that there was another way of handling their trouble.

One could give many instances where family-systems therapy has been helpful. But each family is a unique set of checks and balances, and the variables are almost infinite. The point of the foregoing section is to give readers a realistic expectation as far as what family therapy attempts to do and can do. It attempts not merely to remove the symptoms, but to change the pattern of enmeshment that supports the symptoms. It believes in working with all parts of the family and all aspects of the environment, including schools, jobs, and other health professionals and the therapies they are using. Family therapy is not the answer to every problem, but its message is a hopeful one. It says to individuals, Do not struggle alone to cure your ills; instead, struggle with others *as a family*, looking into yourselves and searching for the answers that surely are there waiting to be found.

9
FAMILY COMMUNICATION

Although as human beings, we come very well equipped for communication, talk between the generations is very difficult. Indeed it is one of the most problematical aspects of family life. Statements like, "I can't talk to you!" "He won't listen to me!" "I don't understand you, you must be crazy!" are common indicators of the mutual incomprehension that seems to be the norm in many families, especially at the time when the offspring are attempting to separate.

A *characteristic of families that communicate well is that family members generally avoid confrontation. Instead of going at each other head to head in situations of potential conflict, it is as if they turn to face the problem together, in a side-by-side position.*

Here I would like to treat the subject of communication in a practical way by citing some of the reasons why we often find it hard to say what we mean, why we sometimes misinterpret what we hear or are misinterpreted by others. It's possible, I think, once we are conscious of the pitfalls, to avoid them and manage to convey clearly what we want to say, as well as to hear and understand better what others are saying.

I would also like to emphasize this basic requirement for improved communication in the family: it is that we always look for the positive reasons for the words and actions of others. If we can start to believe that family members always do what they do for positive reasons (to maintain the family system), then there are positive reasons for their words and actions, however negative their behavior may seem on the surface.

Avoiding Confrontation

A frequent problem in family communication is the *tendency to be confrontational*. A characteristic of families that communicate well is that the family members generally avoid confrontation. Instead of going at each other head to head in situations of potential conflict, it is as if they turn to face the problem together, in a side-by-side position.

Helen and Paula, the mother and daughter mentioned in chapter 1, are a good example of the way communication can collapse into confrontation. Paula, the daughter, had a life pattern of getting a job, disliking it, quitting or being fired, and getting another. Whenever she and her mother got together, the subject would come up and Paula would dominate the conversation by talking about her unhappiness. But it was always her mother who

made the first move by asking, "How are things at work?"
The mother would then criticize and advise ("You never
seem to give things a chance!" "Why do you always pick
the wrong people to work for?" and so forth). Paula would
come back with, "It's my business, I'll take care of it."

Things began to change when someone suggested to
Helen that she see her daughter as usual but without asking the troublesome question. After their next meeting this
small alteration in the communication pattern proved to
have a curious effect, because Helen later heard through
friends that her daughter was hurt and angry rather than
relieved at not being asked about the job.

Systemically, the relationship between this mother and
daughter is very involved, but here we'll confine ourselves
to the aspect of confrontation and how that could be
changed.

This mother felt the need to end the predictable quarrels that happened whenever she saw her daughter. To herself she expressed her stand in words like this: "I am not
going to ask about her job, because that never makes anything better. All it does is cause us to fight, and that makes
me feel ineffectual, like a bad mother. I feel much better
not offering myself up." In this way she took the first step
toward addressing the problem with her daughter in a side-
by-side position, and it put Paula in the position of having
to act instead of *react*.

As with everything that happens in families, Paula's
complaining served an important purpose in maintaining
her family's equilibrium, and once she was deprived of her
cue line, Paula felt bewildered. She had to make her own
adjustment to get into balance with the change her mother
had made. Her way of doing this was to complain to
friends and, in effect, ask her mother through them, "Why
are you doing this?"

In the old state of balance, Paula acted very much as a dependent person (being depressed and losing jobs) and her mother responded to that with displays of aggravation and motherly concern. In the new equilibrium Paula's mother was indicating to her daughter that she no longer needed to be so involved in her daughter's problems.

The script for a situation like the one above might proceed as follows:

Helen, who is the person controlling the situation, figuratively turns aside or turns in the same direction her daughter is going. When Paula says, "I hate my job, I think I'll have to quit," Helen does not answer with one of her usual judgmental responses ("Well, why did you antagonize your boss?"). Instead she might say, "What do you think, Paula? Suppose we walk and talk together and you tell me what you think you should do." In this same way, Helen continues to turn aside every attempt her daughter makes to confront her. Helen may relate a similar situation that happened in her own life and tell what actions she took. However, she leaves it to her daughter to come up with her own choices, which are really the only choices that Paula has available to her.

Elements of the martial defense arts are based on this principle of nonconfrontation, which may partly explain why so many Americans are training in methods like aikido, where the defender uses the strength of the attacker to overcome him. Our own culture seems to value confrontation. We express it in phrases like "eyeball to eyeball," "when push comes to shove." We value physical combativeness in sports like football, basketball, hockey, and now even tennis. However, in personal relationships, confrontation usually produces the opposite of a winning outcome. Good businessmen understand this. They never get stuck in a confrontation that won't pay off; they always provide a way to get around the stalemate.

Some may suggest that confrontation is useful for breaking out of a static situation, for establishing a winner and a loser. This solution is usually more apparent than real, as we see in those marriages where one spouse becomes the victor and the other spouse becomes the vanquished. The vanquishedness of the one spouse may only drive the other one crazy and he or she, too, begins to break down (as Edward Albee clearly depicted in his play *Who's Afraid of Virginia Woolf?*).

No, I find very little to recommend in the idea of confrontation as a catharsis for families. Honesty and clarity, yes, but not in the context of fighting and emotional disturbance.

What I suggest is, I realize, much more difficult than fighting. It is always harder to find and follow the balance between our needs and the needs of others. It is even harder for people to communicate side by side if they come from families where the behavioral norm was conflict and confrontation.

In our efforts to stay out of confrontation, we should try to recognize our indicator of inner conflict—whether it be a churning stomach, a faster heart rate, a clenched jaw, or whatever—and on that signal try to imagine the side-by-side position mentioned above. It's helpful to think of the issue as a kind of destination that you and your would-be confronter will approach together. Elicit the views of the other and whenever you feel that you are coming face to face, move again to that imaginary side-by-side inquiring position. Above all, try not to become the physical embodiment of your opinion in a discussion, so that you start speaking or gesturing angrily. When that happens, communication becomes a battlefield, not a meeting ground.

Saying What You Mean

The inability to speak directly and honestly is another cause of trouble in families. I believe it comes mostly from our misplaced need to protect those we love from painful realities. Children do this, withholding knowledge from their parents so as not to cause them worry and grief. Parents also use this kind of deception for fear that if they are completely truthful, they will damage their children. So they express emotions such as anger, loneliness, and disappointment by half-truths and indirection, holding something back so as to avoid hurting their child.

Indirection may have started with Adam and Eve (I mean, Adam didn't want a bite of the apple, he probably wanted a bite of Eve). And today it has been turned into something of an art form by the advertising industry, which communicates messages to us in terms of exaggeration, double meaning, subliminal images, and selective truth and untruth. To swim against this tide in our own communication is very difficult to do.

Even so, it is always better to say what the situation is and to be honest about the feelings that motivate us. In the following instance, a father spoke out of disappointment and anger but aimed his words wide of the mark.

George Peterson waited for two weeks for a call from his son Gary, who had left the family home in Los Angeles to live and work in San Diego. George and Gary had things to discuss, including what to do with Gary's car, which was sitting in the Petersons' driveway with a broken transmission. As the days passed with no word from his son, George Peterson began to fume. Finally he went to the phone, got the number of the place where Gary worked, and called him up. His opening words were, "I thought you were supposed to call me, Gary!"

"I completely forgot, Dad," Gary answered. "I've been so busy getting settled here."

If George Peterson had spoken plainly from his feelings, he might have said, "Gary, you've left me with a problem and you don't seem to care about it. You said you would call but you didn't, and I think that's pretty inconsiderate of you." Although there would seem to be only a slight difference between "You said you would call, but you didn't" and "I thought you were supposed to call me," the difference is crucial. The first statement is a direct and simple expression of the father's hurt and anger. The second statement leaves him stuck in his anger and leaves the son confused about what his father's message really is.

Of course it is possible for relationships to be upset and seemingly destroyed by directly spoken words, but I have never seen this happen as a result of direct and honest dealings. Many families exist where the members freely express themselves—often bombastically—without damaging their relationships. On the other hand, indirection is frequently a part of dysfunction and disconnection; you need only listen in on a schizophrenic family to hear indirection carried to its most extreme degree.

So once again, it should be stressed that in family life, half-truths and secrets don't work, protection doesn't work. Well-meaning parents who practice this kind of protection with their young children often find that when the time comes to speak with them as adults, it is very difficult to be honest and open. Conversation between them is stilted and avoided when possible.

I don't mean to suggest that directness in speech can be practiced as if it were a simple physical reflex. Our choice of words can make the truth easier or harder to take. But the right words will come more readily when masked emotions are not operating under the surface to confuse the message. As simply as we possibly can, we should try to speak from our real feelings and needs.

The Temptation to Evade

Attempting to evade these needs and feelings is another common pitfall in communication. It happens in every aspect of family life, between parents and children, between siblings, between fathers and mothers. "You know, I *always* like to talk with her," a man said of his wife, "but she always wants to talk late at night, and late at night I'm too tired, I have to go to sleep."

Like this woman, who always picks the wrong time to talk to her husband, we all unconsciously practice evasion. We bring things up at unsuitable times in unsuitable ways, so as to avoid addressing what needs to be addressed, thus keeping things exactly the way they are. If we really talked, it might upset the family homeostasis. In this woman's case, the circumstances are not unusual. She is sliding deeper and deeper into depression. Her two sons are living in apartments of their own and her daughter is away at college. The family activities that formerly absorbed her have suddenly evaporated. The children who'd been home to appreciate her cooking are now eating at other tables, the rooms she enjoyed decorating and freshening are now empty. And her husband has no answer for her depression except to keep bringing it up in the tone of a loving caretaker ("Dear, there must be something we can do to make you less depressed").

Unless this couple can change their pattern of evasion, the situation they are in will become even more difficult to change. Indeed, it can only get worse, and the worsening will complicate the emancipation process of their children. Substituting new patterns of behavior and new means of communication is one of the ways that family therapy can help people in a situation like this. It provides an opportunity for families to meet and talk, and in the talking the members begin to see that they are not isolated in their burdens and unhappinesses but instead are an integral part of a system in which everyone is feeling burdened and uncomfortable to some extent. They all begin to see that this problem they are focusing on is not the problem of a single member but actually is a family problem, something they can change only by working together on it. In the case of the depressed and lonely mother and her husband, this kind of help might enable the wife to act in a different way. She might try, for example, to show that she is capable of taking an interest in her husband's problems. If she could say, "How are things going for you, dear?" the effect might be to make her husband start to feel freer and less burdened and perhaps more available to talk with her about their life together and their problems. There are many ways in which the relationships could start to operate differently, to the benefit of all, but not while the people involved keep finding ways to avoid talking about their joint problem.

Talking and Listening

Another obstacle to communication is the habit which I see in some parents of carrying on nonstop, one-way "conversation" that allows no input from their child. It seems almost as if these parents fear that if they listened for a moment, their children might tell them something they do not want to hear. However, children do find ways of getting their parents' attention. They may get in trouble at school or with the police; they may become depressed or anorectic or pregnant; they may even run away. Of course, there can be other reasons why they do these things, but where they do it out of the need to be heard, it seems a terrible price to pay.

Something else that affects communication is the concern, which we all have, with the way we appear to the outside world. For example, just watch a parent introducing his or her child to another adult. If the child smiles, shakes hands, speaks amiably, and in general reflects well on the parent, that parent's pleasure is evident in his own beaming smile.

Teaching acceptable words and behaviors is part of the process of socializing our children—of making them fit for the company of other human beings—and it is also part of responsible parenting. But sometimes parents seem to put the forms and values of society ahead of their children's needs.

One father broke out of the attitude one night during dinner in a restaurant in the company of his twenty-two-year-old daughter, his new wife, and a group of friends. The conversation took some turn that was upsetting to his daughter and she suddenly burst into tears and ran out of the restaurant. "My God," thought her father, "we're making a scene," and for a moment he was torn between the urge to be a gracious host and the urge to be a father. Then he said to himself, "To hell with what people think or say," and went out of the restaurant to find and comfort his daughter. Afterward he said, "The talk we had was helpful to her, but more so to me."

Sometimes in dealing with their children, parents seem

to forget—or they don't feel bound by—the basic rules of communication, particularly the rule that if we really want to talk with someone, the only thing we should be doing is talking with that person. One executive, I recall, said he thought he spent plenty of time in his son's company, but actually the only time they spent together during the week was on Saturday mornings when the boy rode around with his father in the car, doing weekend chores. It hadn't occurred to this man that he always gave his son a kind of divided attention, something he would never do with his associates at work.

For children to be able to communicate, they need to feel that they are individuals in their own right, not merely representatives of their parents. They respond best when clearly addressed face to face by one person (or parent) at a time.

In communication, talk itself means little. The actions that go with our words are the primary communicators of meaning. For example, a family might be bombastic, contradictory, and pestering in its style of communication, but if you could turn down the sound on that particular family, what you might see would be gestures imbued with warmth and caring.

Parents frequently try to communicate with their child by lecturing and find that their words have little effect. Again, if they want to make a deep and lasting impression, they can only do it by their actions and their behavior toward their child and toward the rest of the world.

Judgmental Words

Judgmental words are another barrier to communication, whether in the family, at work, or at play.

They tend to cut off discussion and cause confrontational attitudes. They function, I believe, as excuses. We tend to use judgmental words rather than push ourselves beyond our everyday ways of thinking, acting, and speaking. It is easier, when we know things are different, to say they are "better" or "worse" rather than find words to express the difference more accurately. It is easier in conversation to say, "You're wrong" when we disagree rather than present a reasoned argument. It is easier to say to a child, "You did a stupid thing" than to help him see his actions as dangerous or harmful to himself or others. (In one family that came for therapy, the father habitually called his son Dummy, and the son was obviously trying to live up to the name.)

In my own life and in my approach to family therapy, I try to stay away from words like *good, bad, right, wrong, better, worse.* (We have tried to do the same in writing this book, with—as you can see—only limited success.) If you can avoid using judgmental words in communicating, your relationships, familial and otherwise, will be much more comfortable and rewarding.

Interpreting Behaviors

The family has been called "a field of misunderstanding on which people at different stages in human development speak to each other with mutual incomprehension,"* and at times we would all be inclined to agree with this unhappy definition.

Misunderstandings are inevitable, I think, until we accept the family as something that operates systemically. We cannot arrive at a satisfactory interpretation of the be-

* Jacques Lacan, as quoted by Richard Sennett in the *New York Times Book Review,* February 24, 1980.

havior of any family member unless we are able to show how that behavior fits in the process of maintaining the family homeostasis.

It ought to be possible for family members to practice positive interpretations of their own and others' actions and to follow up with positive rather than negative responses. We sometimes seem disposed to do this anyway; it is not at all unusual to hear a parent say, "I understand how my child feels, *but* . . ." or for a child to say, "I know what my parents are feeling, *but* . . ."

To further this kind of understanding I propose an exercise I call "charting behaviors." It can be done strictly as a mental process, but if it is also done on paper it has greater value in forcing us to think of possible interpretations and responses. The writing-down is not important in itself; it merely forces us to think of possible positive reasons. This is an extension of what is generally called "trying to see the other person's side" and involves a reversal of viewpoints.

In typical situations of family dis-ease, the parents see their own actions as positive and the child's as negative, while the child sees his parents' behavior as negative and his own behavior as positive. Charting behaviors may help to break this stalemate by an exchange of viewpoints, so that each party to the problem can see how the others are trying to do "their best" in a situation. It can be done by just one person in a family, however, it is much more effective if done by all the members of the family, who then pool their notes together, as in the example that follows.

Problem: Tom wants to bring home his girl friend to spend Thanksgiving at home with his parents. They say they don't think they'll feel comfortable with a stranger in the house, and if she does come, she and Tom will have to sleep in separate rooms. Tom thinks they're being unreasonable.

| | RESPONSE WITH POSITIVE |
| AUTOMATIC RESPONSE *vs.* | INTERPRETATION |

Parents:

"He's putting us in a terrible position. . . . He's too young to be doing this!"

"I guess he's trying to show us he's growing up. . . . And besides, that's the way life is at college."

Tom:

"They want everything *their* way. . . . They can't stand seeing me grow up."

"I guess it's hard for them to share their love for me with a stranger. . . . They're embarrassed to see me having a love affair. . . . It probably makes them feel older."

Charting behaviors is useful for many reasons. In the first place, it helps us to state our problems, which is how we begin to solve them. The solution to our problems is within us, but finding it is complicated by a lack of self-knowledge, among other things. An advantage to charting each other's behavior *as a family* is that each member gains in self-knowledge; each person tries to see himself as he or she is seen by others.

Charting is useful, too, in that it acts as a brake to ill-considered action. It gives parents time to look at the circumstances instead of feeling that they have to react immediately to every situation. Instead, they step back from the situation, discuss it together, and try to think of the possible positive reasons why their child and they are acting in a certain way. (What is it in response to? What is it a search for? If we believe that our child is not doing it to harm the family, then what might the reasons be for his behavior and ours?) Children, of course, can use the same reasoning and the same kind of questions.

Again, I want to stress that in answering these "whys," we have to work from the premise that people in families would always rather be kind to each other. When children don't tell their parents something that has importance in their lives, it is because they feel their parents would be better off without the information than with it. Children don't withhold or lie to hurt their parents; they do it in order to make things easier for them.

Two Devices for Improved Communication

There are two other devices I would like to suggest for improving family communication.

The first is *switching roles*; that is, during part of the time they spend together, each of the family members plays the role of another one. One family I know did this with great success during the years when the children were growing up. Every now and then, at dinner, they would switch places at the table: a child would play the father, another would play the mother, and the parents would play the children. In this way the family members got a remarkable sense of what it felt like to have to deal from each other's positions.

People in families tend to expect certain behaviors, strengths, and responsibilities from each other, without trying to imagine how these attributes arise. The father, for example, is expected to be understanding, wise, just, loving, and so forth. The mother is expected to be all these things as well as tireless, efficient, and accomplished in all the domestic sciences. In reality we are all limited in our ability to have any of those virtues, and switching roles can take us a long way to understanding what it feels like to have these expectations placed on us. Also, it's fun to do.

The second device may be a little harder for families to accept, because it reveals us so powerfully to ourselves. It calls for the use of a tape recorder to reveal patterns of family communication. Every now and then, when the family members are together—at dinner, for example—they leave the machine on the table in the recording mode and forget about it (if they can) while they are eating and talking. At some later time they replay the tape and comment on what they are hearing: Who was heard from and not heard from? Who was repeatedly interrupted—and by whom? Were some things spoken with hidden or double meaning? Did different people interpret the same thing differently? What were the varied responses of people around the table?

This device is capable of showing us things we may not be ready to see or hear, and therefore I think it is appropriate only for families who feel they want to try it and only at the times when all are agreed on doing it. For those who employ it, taping can be very useful. Most of us at times say things with absolutely no cognizance of the response we are causing in others. As a way of showing how families communicate, taping can be a real eye-opener.

I have tried to present some of the many things we can do to monitor and improve family communication. Certainly, if a family feels dis-eased in its ability to communicate, it is time for a change. Though this will not be easy to do, it is worth the effort for the ease it can bring us.

10

DEPENDENTLY
INDEPENDENT: THE
FAMILY ENDURES

In the fifteen years since her husband died Muriel Stone seemingly hasn't had a worry in the world. The massive heart attack that unexpectedly claimed her husband left her in the care of her son, Howard, "a wonderful son," as she is fond of calling him. And, it must be said, Howard *is* exceptional. Precociously canny in business, he was rich before the time he was twenty-five and has been the mainstay of his mother's life throughout her widowhood. He speaks to her almost every day, sees her once or twice a week, and makes sure she wants for nothing. She has, she says, a "rich and full" life, which consists of keeping up her friendships, doing volunteer work one day a week, traveling occasionally, and taking her two little grandchildren on outings in the city. Her friends all say what a wonderful story it is, that after being dependent on his parents during the years of his upbringing, Howard was ready to take on responsibility when that was needed and to be the one his mother could depend on.

But there is another side to Muriel's story: she is sixty years old and she has been taken care of in this way since she was forty-five. The self-supporting job she might have

taken and succeeded at, the second marriage she might
have made had she been able to consider it, these and all
the other aspects of the life she might have made for herself can now only be unanswered questions in her mind.

Howard and his mother, with all the best intentions,
have managed to derail the process of mutual growth and
separation, and although the situation is far from hopeless,
it would be much harder for them to change their lives
now than it would have been fifteen years ago.

Throughout this book we have tried to show that the
emancipation of an offspring is an evolutionary process
that begins at birth and is helped along by a family atmosphere in which there is

- openness, rather than secrecy;
- guidance by parameters that the parents agree on and
consistently observe;
- the allowance (if not actually the encouragement) of
mistakes and failures as a necessary part of the maturation process;
- an example, set by the parents, that change and adjustment to circumstances are possible at any point in life;
and
- resolution and growth of family relationships so that
members are able to move on to lives and families of
their own instead of getting "stuck" in patterns of family interdependency.

We come now to the stage in family life where it becomes evident whether that evolution has gone well or less
than well—as in the case of Howard Stone and his mother.
(The enmeshment that binds these two together might
not have happened if the mother had been able to adjust
more creatively to her aloneness, and if her son had been

less influenced by a familial pattern that cast him early in life as the successful, dependable one.) Awareness of the pitfalls in the emancipation process may help families to avoid them and move on to the next stage of family life, a stage in which the generations will be connected but not tied to each other, in which the young will enjoy their freedom while their parents will enjoy the lightening of their responsibilities, in which the two generations will be supportive of each other without being dependent, in which the parent will become the resourcer, storyteller, and sage, while the independent offspring will become a link to the renewing cycle of life and family.

Emancipation Is Mutual

Separation, emancipation, freedom, independence—whatever word we apply to the process whereby a young person begins to act on his or her own, they all mean that a kind of distance opens up between the parents and the child. It may or may not be an actual geographical distance, but in all cases it is an emotional distance.

This process of distancing begins, as we have said, at birth, when the baby emerges into the world and begins to move outward from the womb to the breast, from the crib to the yard to the school, with each step moving more and more out of physical contact with his parents. The period of emancipation, when the child actually begins to live without parental protection and support, usually is the period when the two generations are most distant from each other. Then—ideally—as the parents enter old age, there is a narrowing of the distance as the child finds ways to be supportive of his parents during this difficult time of life. Such a progression would be "perfect" distancing. Unfortunately, however, it doesn't happen this way with any great frequency. Instead, we often see families where the paths of parents and child continue closely parallel for the lifetime of one or both parents, or where the paths diverge with no narrowing of the gap during the declining years when the parents feel the need to be closer to their children.

In a well-functioning family, the healthy emotional distance is not much affected by great geographical distance. Parents may live in Florida or Arizona and their children someplace far away, but the distance need not make a change in their emotional connectedness. The family members use whatever means they can—letters, phone calls, visits—to express their continuing relationship.

What I have described may sound like a process in which at one point or another both generations begin to interact together as equals. Yet this never seems to happen. There always seems to be an inequality in the relationship between a parent and his or her child. The two generations remain aware of who is parent and who is child and this awareness affects every transaction between them. This holds true even in families where the generations have switched roles, so to speak, with the child becoming the chief support of an aged and dependent parent. I have seen fifty- and sixty-year-old men suddenly seem more like twelve-year-olds when in the presence of their octogenarian mother or father.

Rebalancing After Separation

As its history progresses, then, a family stays in balance by the shifting of dependencies from one generation to the next. That is a long view of family homeostasis, however. If we look at equilibrium in its momentary sense (the family is in balance at all times), the question is, How does the family come back into balance at the time the child moves out and his dependency is no longer such a heavy factor in the family homeostasis?

The answer is that the missing factor has to be replaced by something. If the child makes his independence moves and the family does not respond in ways that help it to form a new equilibrium with the child in the new position, then the pull on the child will always be to come back.

Although I have made this point in many earlier examples, it comes true so often, so stunningly, that it bears repeating here. For example, I am thinking of Molly, a young woman whose family I know socially. Her parents' policy on raising children was to pay all expenses through college but to turn the spigot off on graduation day; from that day on the kids were supposed to make their own way. After getting her degree, Molly moved 1,500 miles away, to Dallas, where she found a job almost immediately. But she felt unattached and depressed in Texas, and meanwhile her parents, at home, were turning more and more to drink to solace themselves in her absence. No one adjusted well to this sudden change; instead of being liberating, it resulted in a strong pull on everyone for Molly to come home.

Many families are able to rebalance after such a drastic change as this. With the proper evolutionary history, a family can accept the children going far beyond easy visiting distance to establish their own life, work, and families. The evolutionary aspect means that they have already spent time apart, physically and emotionally, before the actual and symbolic act of separation. When that moment comes, they are able to find different ways of relating and to fill the empty place with things that are as fulfilling to them as the closeness they previously enjoyed.

The separation or moving-out of a member, if and when

it is accepted, truly changes the life of everybody else in the system.

It may not be too extreme to take the example of a house of cards. In a child-centered family, if you remove the foundation-level card (child), then the house falls and has to be reassembled into a different model where that foundation member comes back into the structure not in a bottom position but at one of the topmost levels, where it is possible to take the card away and put it back without radically changing the structure of the house (family). The child becomes importantly peripheral, a "visiting card" rather than a foundation card. If there are no other children, the basic structure, to remain viable, becomes a simple A-frame made of mother and father, who make a relationship that fits the new circumstances and is supportive for both of them. The children, when visiting, are really add-ons rather than supportive members.

From my observation, the parents who are best able to build two-member structures after their children are gone are those who have a strong sense of their individuality. They don't wait on their children. They do not evaluate themselves according to their children's success or seeming lack of it. They have lives of their own and are involved in activities they like. Again, this is usually an evolutionary process; parents who, in their earlier years, never enjoyed friendships or sports or crafts or career interests may find it hard to fill the voids created when their children leave.

It has to be remembered, then, that the work of emancipation belongs as much to the parent as to the child. There has to be *a mutual separation*.

What we see in many cases is that the parents (one or both) are not able to make a successful transition and become disturbed and nonfunctioning in some way; often they become depressed. Especially in the traditional family, it is often the mother who does this. She may try to live as if her children still needed her as a provider, whereas the number of times they really need her are very few. She may lie to herself and to her husband that her life is full, but they see that her life is empty. The children come home more often than they would like and they come with the lie that they are there only because they want to come. Their growth is restricted by their sense of responsibility, and, sadly, their attempts to help their mother have the opposite effect, since they tend to confirm the mother's belief that she is still needed as a nurturer. The traditional helping moves the family makes tend to keep the situation more or less as it is. The parent can only continue to signal her (or his) deterioration by a worsening condition (such as inertia, fear of going out, physical illness), because the issues of why she is unhappy and how she can change seem impossible to deal with.

Children Who Stay Home

The problem of the young person who cannot separate, or the one who returns home after a first foray into the world, is frequently tied to the problem of parental inability to adjust to the transition.

I am not speaking about every young person who is still home at the age of, say, twenty-five. There is no bracketable "transition period" as such; every family has its own timetable. In some families the child never moves out or never gets entirely free of family enmeshment.

The reasons why a child stays home usually are disguised. Reasons commonly given are that the parents need the income the child provides, or that the child is not yet

financially ready to live independently; sometimes graduate
school is used as a way to postpone leaving.

When a grown child stays home, in most cases it is not
because of the stated reasons but because the family has
needs that the child fulfills by staying where he is. The parents, for their part, may complain about their grown children who are still "hanging around the house," taking
"meaningless" jobs, or perhaps remaining frankly on the
dole, yet the truth of the matter may be that the children
are staying home, or staying on the dole, not because they
want to sponge off the parents (they are as unhappy about
the situation as are their parents), but because their families need them to be in that position.

So, then, when a child cannot move out it is a sign of a
needy system, and it behooves families in these situations
to ask themselves what needs that child is serving by staying home. The mother who says facetiously "I hate them"
of her grown sons who are still at home is speaking from
inside a tightly knit relationship in which both sides are
ready to scream; if you could ask the sons, they'd probably
say the same thing of their mother. But "hating" is not
what is going on in that household. Rather, it is the need
of the children to keep their mother "hating" them—to use
her word—because they fear that if they were to leave her
alone she would fall prey to worse things than her unhappiness at having to put up with them.

Sometimes, by getting into trouble, a child makes his or
her life into something the parent can focus on in place of
whatever frightening and necessary life change the parent
faces. With the best possible intentions, the child puts off
that reckoning for the parent, but in reality he is not helping. This "solution" is not a solution, since the troublesome issues in the parent's life—the unhappiness, the am-

bivalence, the unresolved past relationships—continue to operate disturbingly under the surface.

Resolving Family Relationships

What is there in the world that compares to the process of bringing up a family? What else is so complex and so all-absorbing? In a war, you might be wounded, or captured, and so get out of the obligation to serve. But not so in the family; *there is no way to get out.* Once you have a child you are forever involved in that expanded system—for better or worse, richer or poorer, in sickness and in health. To expect that the parenting will end with the coming of age of the children is unrealistic. And the same condition holds for the children. Those who say, "I'm separated from my family, I no longer talk to them, and I like it this way" reveal by their vehemence or sadness the presence of unresolved ties that have not been lived out and brought to ease.

The more I see, the more convinced I become that our ability to live and function is governed by how well we evolve our family relationships. If we don't resolve them, we cannot be content with our lives. We cannot form a new marriage unless we are comfortable with the dissolution of any previous marriage. We cannot raise children to the state of functioning independence until we understand how our own parents "did their best" in raising us. We can attempt these moves, but as long as we are disconnected and uncomfortable with our familial past, ease will elude us. There will be a sadness and an incompleteness in our lives, however much we may try to hide it from view. No length of time in psychoanalysis or any other therapy will give us the comfort we seek unless we have made our participation in the family system one in which there are no black holes, voids, or breaks in the wiring. The connectors have to be reconnected—not closely or tightly, but comfortably. The voids have to be filled, because a void can never be comfortable. (Witness the attempts of adopted children to find out about their biological parents—who they were, what they looked like and acted like, where they are, and what became of them.) There is no ease possible in a complete break from family.

This is not to say that those of us who are disconnected in some degree from our families have to resign ourselves to being dis-eased for the rest of our lives. We can work on reconnecting and getting comfortable with our past, even with family members who are no longer alive.

Seeing and recognition—whereby we get a truer understanding of ourselves and the other members of our family —are first steps in the process of resolving relationships. Sometimes recognition comes in a flash, as it did to a man of thirty-five during a weekend visit to his parents. "I have always thought of my father as a very strong person," he said later, "but watching him at dinner I realized that behind all his determination and self-discipline, he is really a very frightened and insecure person. I felt as if my childhood ended at that moment."

What we see depends on how open we are to this kind of revelation, particularly to seeing how the generations mirror one another. We have spoken earlier about generational patterns—how influential they are and how difficult they are to change. Our attitudes—toward marriage, work, play, limits—carry on basic similarities learned from our families of origin. It's almost as if we were carbon copies, *but in disguise*. (I have heard a man call his wife by his deceased mother-in-law's name—which may seem strange, except that frequently, as a wife grows older, her resemblance to the way her mother looked and behaved at the same age becomes more and more pronounced.)

Parents may not recognize how much their children resemble them, or how much *they* resemble their own parents. Young adults may continue to see their parents as gods until the day when they finally see them as human beings, and then they may feel disillusioned, unless they understand (which they rarely do) how much their parents fit the mold of the family generational patterns. Maturity cannot occur until children are able to appreciate and accept their own resemblance to their parents. Having myself accepted the uncomfortable truth of this mirroring process, I find the resemblances in my own and other families that I know well to be clearer the better I know the people; their generational values and norms usually are remarkably similar.

As it is, we are only imperfectly able to see the resemblances, and to see ourselves as we are and others as they are. We see ourselves as we *wish* we were—or as our parents wished we would be. We speak proudly of our children following in our footsteps and we concentrate on the positives of that transference; we forget that they cannot have the positives unless they also take on the negatives of the transference—the insecurities and lack of fulfillment or accomplishment that we, like most people, have been willing to live with.

Each generation gives birth to its monuments. The monuments that make us feel good about ourselves are the ones we like to have on display in our home. The monuments that disturb us are the ones we put in the closet. But they don't hide very well; they haunt us, we hear the screams coming out of the closet.

I don't use this harsh metaphor thoughtlessly. So much of family unhappiness must be laid to the closing of doors, to the reluctance of family members to look at themselves. The hoped-for change lies in family members opening those doors. They need to look at their relationships with themselves, their antecedents, their siblings, and their progeny, and they need to address the unresolved issues that exist in their own unique family system.

This is not by any means a simple matter. When there is distance existing between family members, it is precisely the distance that allows them to be comfortable in their uncomfortableness with each other. If there is anger between siblings, it persists because the system has gotten used to that anger being there. The removal of the anger is not just a matter of reconciliation, but a matter of systemic adjustment.

Let's step back from abstraction at this point and remind ourselves that families consist of human beings made of flesh and blood. We need to be able to see and accept that humanity.

Seeing has to do with children growing up and seeing their parents as they are—liver spots and all—and accepting their parents as less than perfect. It has to do with the parents being their real selves with their children, even if it means letting the imperfections show. (On a trip abroad my wife and I met for the first time the mother of a woman we both know. We were astonished that the woman we saw and spoke to and the woman described by her daughter seemed to be two different people. I am constantly amazed at the way a child's perception of his or her parents can be so widely at odds with the reality.)

Seeing has to do with parents accepting their children as individuals with positive and negative qualities that mirror their own. (In this connection, another woman we know had a funny moment of revelation the day she took her daughter for her first gynecological examination. When

one is angry, it is better to express the anger. What I
ying is, *don't get angry*. If you feel the emotion stir-
teer the conversation toward something you can talk
that will not trigger the usual dispute. Focus on con-
the physical manifestation of your anger; that way
l be able to control both the anger and the conver-

*you resolve relationships in a family where there
eem to be anyone left to connect with?*
uch harder to do, but it's do-able. If your parents
and there are no siblings, there are almost always
cles, cousins, even close friends, neighbors, or
ciates with whom you could talk.
ive far away from these people, you could estab-
connections by letter (the same is true for family
ho live at a distance). People like to get letters
ike to reminisce about the past. Ask them to
and help you get a sense of your parents—how
what their experiences were, what they were
o helpful to study old letters, diaries, and fam-
nd try to get close to the people who wrote
nd posed for those pictures.

lt Feelings of Parents and Children

vhat transpires between parents and their
has to do with feelings of guilt.
"My kid is not going to amount to any-
y feel guilty that their marriage has not pro-
ms to them to be a perfect product.
"I am doing this [or "not doing this"] for
ause I feel guilty. I'm damned if I do and
't."

the girl thought that she might have to undress in front of
the doctor, she was frantic with embarrassment—not that
she would be seen without clothes on, but that she was
wearing cotton panties, which would make her seem a
mere child. She begged her mother to take off her own
sexy underwear and trade with her right there in the doctor's office. My friend was ready to cite her daughter for
vanity until she realized that her daughter was only em-
ulating her.)

When we are able to see and accept a truer picture of
ourselves and our family members, we can get on with the
work of resolving familial relationships.

In the course of this book we have discussed many people who are "stuck" in problematic relationships with important family figures: they have the choice of getting "un-
stuck" or else settling for lives less fulfilled and less
effective than they might be. The work of resolving relationships, "connecting back," as we have called it, is a kind
of pilgrimage in which we go in search of ourselves. Perhaps the best way to describe it is in question-and-answer
form.

What is the object of connecting back?
It is to form comfortable connections with the members
of your family, so that you can feel at ease (not necessarily
great or very good) about them, whether you are with
them or are only in communication with them. Often this
means changing a relationship in which you now feel very
uncomfortable.

Whom do I talk to, and how many times?
Ask yourself first, Where are the known disconnections?
Is it with your father, brother, sister, or mother? Take

them on one at a time, beginning with the one who is easiest to approach. Your first conversation should be brief. You can be frank in saying that there is an area of your life —a broken or uncomfortable connection—where you would like to feel more at ease. Meet and talk with that person as many times as you need to in order to bring that feeling of greater ease about. When you think you have made progress, you can go on to more difficult relationships and proceed in the same way.

What do we talk about?

Do not use reproaches, recriminations, blame, or confrontation. Generalities of that sort never work. Let's say a grown woman goes to her older brother and says, "I'm still mad because when we were little you always hogged the television set and now I want to talk to you about that." Her brother will say, "Like hell, I never hogged the television set! You always used to leave the bathroom dirty and I could never get you off the toilet, and I don't want to talk about it anyway. You were the one that was wrong!" That's a good way to keep the relationship exactly where it is. So don't come to these conversations itching to drag out your old resentments.

Proceed instead by trying to recall together what happened in early years between the two of you. Talk about your family history. Try to put yourself in the place of the person you are talking to. Suppose you are talking to an older brother. Ask him what it was like in the family before you were born, or about a house your family once lived in that you never saw, or a relative whom you were too young to know before he or she died. Compare notes on your family tree.

How can we avoid getting ang do that anyway?

If confrontation seems to drifting toward a subject the "get into," except perhaps t *from that subject.* If the o *you* seem to want to talk prefer to stay with what we me more stories about G other still comes at you in ing. When he stops doin you can begin again to pr

The person who is a tions has to remain in sation; this is essential. ting out an agenda pronouncements abor It means making s velop so that it rein disconnection. (I a her mother and br her husband cam read it together, mother about al wronged her. I very well. If yo you don't do i and agreed wi that didn't o ing back are everyone spi ter for hav don't feel

How ca doesn't

It's m are dead aunts, u work asso

If you lish those members and they write to yo they lived, like. It is al ily albums those words

Gu
Much of grown childrer
Parents say, thing," and th duced what see
Children say my parents bec damned if I dor

when am sa ring, s about trolling you wi sation.

These are just two of the many typical statements one hears from parents and children expressing the dis-ease that deprives them of mutual joy and satisfaction in their relationship.

Writings about guilt in popular literature usually stress the unprofitability of guilt feelings but tell little about how to handle the issues that underlie these feelings. We cannot simply walk away from these issues without feeling just that much more guilty for having done so. Nor should we accept guilt and live with it, because it *is* an unprofitable feeling.

Guilt feelings serve a definite purpose in people's lives, but not necessarily as a way of expiating crimes. (How many people who feel burdened with a sense of guilt could point to any crime they have committed that could account for their unhappiness?) No, I believe that when we keep guilt in our relationships, it is because we don't know any better way to handle our problems. I spoke with a mother who told me how dissatisfied she and her husband were with the nonproductive aspects of their son's life (he'd just had his second successive failure in business). "You know," she said, "I've figured out that it's my husband who's responsible for our son not knowing how to make a go of things. I used to feel guilty about it, but I don't want to feel that way anymore. I think he's to blame and now that I think that I feel much better."

I asked her how come that let her off the hook since, after all, she chose her husband and married him and had children with him.

"No, no," she insisted, "it's *his* fault."

Setting aside the larger, systemic question of how their son's repeated "failures" might have served the needs of this family, it is striking the way this mother insisted on blaming her husband. Somehow, by assigning the guilt to him she found an "explanation" for the family problem and this allowed her to keep the *status quo* rather than search for better solutions.

Another very common expression of guilt feelings is the statement of the adult child who says, "I guess I should see more of my parents and talk to them more. When I call up and my mother says, 'I hope you'll come be with us for at least a week,' I feel awful. I mean, I only get two weeks and it's really dull where they are."

What a statement like this expresses is not so much the child's unwillingness to be bored as his sadness that he will find his parents older, feebler, and more needy—as well as his fear that he will not be able to cope well with their change.

Actions done out of guilt provide a false sense of "payoff" at best, not any real satisfaction in getting comfortable in a relationship. When children are more attentive to their parents because they would feel guilty if they weren't, these transactions are empty of real warmth and affection.

As with every problem in parent-child relationships we have discussed so far, guilt is an evolutionary problem and the solutions are evolutionary solutions. There are no pills for immediately relieving the pain.

A frequent source of guilt feelings in families is the investment parents have in their children: if the parents don't see their children "succeeding" (in the parents' terms), they consider themselves to be failures as parents. For this reason, many parents continue to advise and censure their grown children, as if by doing so they could turn them onto the path of success. I think one of the reasons children avoid spending time with their parents is that when the two generations are together, there is the feeling that the parents must parent their children, even though the children may be thirty, forty, or fifty years old. The interaction between the generations—in the subjects that come up and the ways they are dealt with—is parent-to-child instead of parent-to-*adult* child.

One of the reasons parents have difficulty accepting their children as capable adults is that the parents have difficulty accepting *themselves* as capable adults. Because they doubt their own "maturity," they can't accept the maturity of their children. If the two generations aren't able to get past this, they tend to stay in the familiar state, where the parent is the grown-up and the child is the child, and the parent continues to help the child so that the child doesn't learn what it's like to be without the parent until it is too late and the parent is gone.

For parents in this situation, I think a most important step is that they try to accept their grown child as a fully capable adult who possesses unique qualities and is doing as well as he or she can at that time in life.

A way of handling guilt—and this applies to both generations—is to respond in those situations that habitually produce guilt feelings with specific different behaviors. In the previous chapter, we talked about a problem of communication between a woman and her daughter. The daughter's life pattern of losing jobs had the mother feeling guilty and, of course, angry at feeling guilty. The move that helped to get this situation off center was for the mother to change her role in their conversations and to stop feeding her daughter the line ("How's your job?") that always triggered the tale of woe. That's a good example of a specific change in behavior that helps reduce guilt feelings. The mother changed her way of speaking about the problem, sounding more like a friend than a censuring, advising parent.

How might children handle a situation where they feel

guilty because they do not see or speak to their parents as much as the parents would like?

One way is to put themselves in their parents' place and to try to see what it is their parents are really saying. When parents let their children know directly or indirectly that they are missing them, the children, it seems to me, often misread the message. What the parents want and need is not really the companionship of the children; if they were able to speak more truly from their feelings, they would say to their children, "I feel lonely, there's not enough going on in my life," rather than, "I wish you'd stop by more often" or "Why don't you come to see me?"

Now, not all parents and grandparents are lonely. Many have evolved full, satisfying lives and they are able to be philosophical about the signs of advancing age, their friends who are dying, and the like. They have made their own separation moves and have lessened their need to be in frequent communication with their children. Their lack of neediness is unconsciously transmitted to their children in the way they speak to them, and the children as a result feel comfortable even when they don't talk to their parents regularly. However, parents who are less well equipped for this life stage often suffer from a sense of emptiness and inactivity.

It is one of the functions of the family that its members help one another, and in the situation of lonely, underactive parents there are specific behaviors the children can undertake to help the problem that both generations are struggling with.

Sometimes all that is needed to help parents get into new activities is encouragement by their children. Travel clubs, book discussion groups, theater outings, adult education classes, arts and crafts exhibitions, photography workshops, and bridge and Scrabble clubs are the kinds of activities that go on in almost every community, and usually the simple act of making a couple of phone calls is all that is necessary for people to get involved. Town recreation departments exist at taxpayers' expense precisely to help members of communities lead healthy, active lives, and the child who wants to help a parent meet people and have fun can begin by contacting that source of information. The point is, there are countless solutions to every problem *if only we begin to think about them.* If you noticed, none of these suggestions involve the child getting into a routine of visiting or scheduled activities—although it is nice when parents and their grown children can enjoy each other's company.

When children try to help their parents in these ways they shouldn't expect the improvement to go like clockwork. Anything that involves changing a set mode of existence is likely to be met with a certain amount of resistance, so the children should be prepared to use diplomacy and quiet persistence if necessary. I think, though, that when parents see that a child is truly trying to help, it makes them feel gratified that their message is getting through and more receptive to practical suggestions.

Guilt is nothing more than an excuse, something we use as a way of dealing with problems. Yet we can't simply dispense with guilt. If we wanted to live without it we would have to try to understand how our system works without "guilt" being needed to explain it. We would have to find more rewarding ways to go about the same daily jobs and relationships.

Once parents and their grown children learn to live and relate at a comfortable distance from one another, they should regard the distance as a kind of fragile achievement, something they have to be careful to preserve if they are not to revert to the old relationship of parent-to-child, child-to-parent. There is always that pull the system exerts to keep things the way they are—for the parents to remain parents and children to remain children. But the need to maintain the distance should not prevent parents from relating to their children in helpful ways. Parents often ask whether they should help their children with their debts and if so to what extent; whether they should pay their children's transportation for visits home; whether and how much they should involve themselves in the raising of grandchildren, and so forth.

Once again, if we focus on the specifics of the question we get nowhere. Where there are uncertainties like this, they are a residue of a growth process that has only partially evolved, and that is where attention should be focused, not on the question itself. The level of comfort between parents and children is a good indicator of how far helping can go.

For example, suppose parents have a child who has left home and gone to live and work in another city. He is earning enough money to have his own home and a reasonably good life but he is not able to afford trips back to the family home. If the parents would like to have that child with them for a visit, and if the child would like to come, then the transaction can be a simple one:

"Can you come for Thanksgiving? We'd love it if you could."

"Well, I'd love to come except I don't see how I can, with all the expenses I'm carrying right now."

"Well, that's all right. We'll send you the ticket. It'll be our pleasure."

An exchange like that presumes the parents can afford to pay the expenses and that the reunion will be a comfortable, satisfying occasion for all.

When parents ask whether or not to pay for trips home, I think often it is more truly a question of whether the family really wants to get together at that time, or whether they think they should get together out of a sense of duty. If they are going to get joy out of the reunion, there should be no problem about whether or not to come or about who should pay. But where there is hardship, or discomfort, or a sense of coercion, then the visit probably should be postponed.

Grandparenting

The grandparenting role, which has much to contribute to family life, is something of a casualty in modern America. In a great many families, the unit of parents and children and grandchildren, which years ago lived within a fairly circumscribed area, has been broken apart. Grandparents live in communities for seniors, often far away from their children, and may see their grandchildren relatively few times in the fleeting years it takes those children to grow up.

Some may say that it's probably better for the grandparents to live where they cannot interfere with the upbringing of the grandchildren, which is sometimes a source of trouble in families. Nevertheless, I think this dispersion has been an unfortunate thing for our society, because our family is one of the few safe harbors that can exist for us in this stormy world.

In those families where grandparents fasten too much on the advisory role, or where they seek to influence the marriage one way or another, perhaps it is because they have not yet learned to accept their children as adults who should be free to raise a family to the best of their ability. It may be also that their lives are not sufficiently filled with friendships and activities that could involve them elsewhere.

When the relationship of grandparents to their children and grandchildren is relatively free of tension, I believe it is full of possibilities for growth. To a child, the grandparent is someone with a fund of stories and experience, someone who is philosophical about life and often available when his parents are involved with their work. For the grandparent, there is the fun of being with a growing child without having the trauma and responsibility of managing the child day in and day out. Baby-sitting works well if the grandparents are available, willing, and able and if their parent children do not presume too much on that availability. It can be a saving thing for young parents who are feeling the stresses of working and child-rearing in a time of economic pressure.

Society would gain immeasurably, I think, if it could find a way to put grandparents solidly back in the family system.

The Extended Household

One way the generations are spending more time in each other's company is through the spreading phenomenon of the *extended household*. Instead of setting up homes of their own separate from their parents, growing numbers of young people are choosing to return to or remain under the parental roof, either singly or with families of their own.

How is this different from the situation where a child stays on because his or her separation has failed to evolve, especially since in both situations the stated reason is often one of economic necessity?

Families where young people are stuck and unable to

separate are usually characterized by an atmosphere of un-freedom and enmeshment. On the contrary, well-function-ing extended households are characterized by the freedom of the members to honor their own needs. Members of two, three, and four generations can live together success-fully if they all follow certain rules governing their physical surroundings and emotional involvements so that each one can enjoy a fair share of "territory" without impinging on others. What may be sacrificed in the extended household, however, is some degree of the individuation process, since when people live close together it is harder for them to evolve their own personalities and life-styles.

It may take some trial and error to arrive at the ground rules for extended-household living. This was the case with Ted Sweet and his parents. Ted is a young electrician who moved his wife and baby from their apartment over a vil-lage store to the unused ell wing of his parents' New En-gland farmhouse; he saw the move as a way to save money so that he and his wife could eventually buy a home of their own. Ted's parents were both about sixty-five at the time of the move, and the constant presence of a lively in-fant began to wear on them after a few months, as did the inevitable collisions over kitchen use. One day, after ten-sions had risen to a certain level, a sudden argument broke out that brought resentments into the open. A few days later, a more level-headed family discussion followed in which the four adults let their needs be known and new ground rules were worked out.

According to these, Ted's parents were assured certain hours of privacy and quiet, and Ted agreed to build a small kitchen in the ell with second-hand appliances and materials that his father would pay for.

Today the Sweets are beginning to get comfortable with each other and the new lease on life is beginning to show

Connectedness means that we grow up in our family, separate out our individuality, and, in time, join or form another family while continuing in a relationship of maturity and adulthood with our family of origin. That is the goal of family life.

in tangible ways. For example, the garden, which was getting smaller year after year, is back to its old, generous dimensions, thanks to the enthusiasm of Ted's wife.

The Sweet family may be small as extended households go, but it is a fairly happy one and illustrates how this arrangement can benefit all the generations.

The extended household is nothing new. It has been a human institution for thousands of years and in societies all over the world. It was part of American life too, but we got away from it in the belief that it was something less than healthy. We took separation to be the ultimate goal of families.

I believe that the ultimate goal of families is not separation but, rather, a comfortable connectedness. For parents, this means being available to their child as experienced human beings who have lived many more years; who have love for their child; who can give that child a shoulder to cry on or a sounding board for ideas or a quiet place when he or she needs some peace; who can be a backup when life gets too complicated or difficult; who can be a translator when life becomes too baffling.

For the offspring, connectedness means growing up in one's family, then separating out one's individuality, and finally combining into a new relationship with other families while continuing in a relationship of maturity and adulthood with one's family of origin. That, I think, is the ultimate goal of family life and the goal that every family should work toward.

INDEX

saying what you mean,
172–74
and side-by-side approach to
family peace, 19
talking and listening, 175–77
Compatibility, marriage, 91–94
Confidence, as parental need in
transitional years, 44–45
Confrontation, and
communication, 168–72
Connecting back, 94–96
Contract, written, in evolving
family ease, 38–39

Decision-making, in
single-parent families,
111–13
Dependent independence. *See*
Independence
Depression, in young adults,
146–49
Dis-ease
and evolving ease, 37–41
family, in adolescence, 27–29
of sane vs. insane, 146
Divorce, 103–4
and family survival, 104–6
and re-forming family, 106–9
Dress, of adolescents, 26–27
Dropping out, 62–63
Drug-taking, 153–55

Elopement, and rites of
passage, 96–97
Emancipation, mutuality of,
185–86
Empty-nest syndrome, and
equality, 123
Energy, of adolescence, 25
Equality, 119–20

establishing, 121–27
and family peace, 18
and financially irresponsible
child, 135–39
and first jobs, 133–35
money and family system,
127–33
Evasion, and communication,
174–75
Expectations, and family peace,
18–19
Experimentation
adolescent, 29–32
and family peace, 17–18
Extended household, 206–9

Failure vs. success, for new
adults, 72–75
Family
and children who stay home,
189–91
and connecting back, 94–96
dis-ease and its function,
27–29
and divorce, 104–6
evolving ease in, 37–41
extended household, 206–9
formation of, 2–8
guilt feelings in, 198–205
and grandparenting, 205–6
independence and endurance
of, 183–85
and mutuality of
emancipation, 185–86
"normal" vs. "abnormal,"
143–46
planning for college, 49–52
rebalancing after separation,
186–89

and formation of new family,
2–8
less than, 97–101
past patterns and future
compatibility, 91–94
and wedding as rite of
passage, 96–97
and young love, 85–87
Money
and family system, 127–33
and financially irresponsible
child, 135–39
and planning for college,
50–51

Oppositional behavior, and
family system, 14–15

Parents
anxiety over new adults,
77–79
and children's oppositional
moves, 14–15
children's protection of,
114–16
and cohabiting children,
97–101
of divorcing partners, 108–9
helping vs. hindering in
school experience, 59–62
need for confidence in
transitional years, 44–45
and success or failure of new
adults, 62–65
see also Single parent
Peace, in family, 17–19
Planning, for college, 49–52
Problems
arising at school, 48–49

intractable, and Thinking the
Unthinkable, 18

Recordings, and
communication, 181–82
Re-formation of family after
divorce, 106–9
Resiliency in family, and
resolving disputes, 40–41
Return, resisting pull on new
adults to, 75–77
Role switching, and
communication, 181
Runaways, 149–53

Sabbaticals, student, 64–65
School experience, 47–48
boarding schools, 56–57
dropping out, 62–64
and family planning for
college, 49–52
and independence, 52–56
parents' helping vs.
hindering, 59–62
and problems at school,
48–49
student sabbaticals, 64–65
vacation times, 57–59
Self-maintaining behaviors,
systemic, 146
Sennett, Richard, 178n
Separation
and family system, 14–17
rebalancing after, 186–89
Sex
extramarital, 82–85
and single parent, 116–18
Sexual mores, and young love,
87–90
Sexual sleep-over, 87–89